CASTING DOWN

DISRUPTIVE IMAGINATIONS

My precious Son,

May this book bless you beyond human words.

Love you.

Mom

DR. SANDRA OGUNREMI

Trilogy Christian Publishers
A Wholly Owned Subsidiary of Trinity Broadcasting Network
2442 Michelle Drive
Tustin, CA 92780

For information, address Trilogy Christian Publishing
Rights Department, 2442 Michelle Drive, Tustin, Ca 92780.
Trilogy Christian Publishing/ TBN and colophon are trademarks of Trinity Broadcasting Network.

For information about special discounts for bulk purchases, please contact Trilogy Christian Publishing.

Manufactured in the United States of America

10 9 8 7 6 5 4 3 2 1

Library of Congress Cataloging-in-Publication Data is available.

ISBN 978-1-64773-524-1 (Print Book)
ISBN 978-1-64773-525-8 (ebook)

Father, I thank you for everything! Thank you for the power to cast down every imagination and high thing that refuses to submit to Your authority. It is with much pleasure that I dedicate this work to You.

—Dr. Sandra Ogunremi

CONTENTS

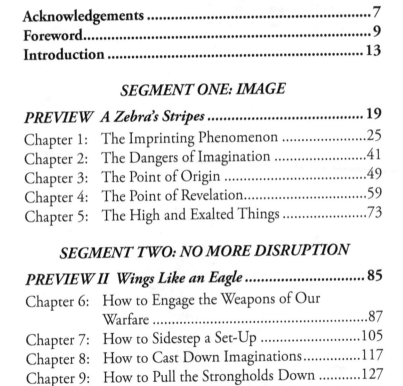

ACKNOWLEDGEMENTS

To my precious husband and covering, Dr. Ayodele Ogunremi: your steadfastness, love, and care are beyond what I can express in human words. Thank you for demonstrating the love of Christ in our lives! Thank you for loving us well. I love you!

To my adult children: it has been a great joy raising you! I love you and I'm proud to be your mom!

To my mother, brother, and sister: I love you! We've weathered storms that have made our commitment to God great!

To my spiritual parents, Revs. George and Oloruntoyin Adegboye: I am forever grateful; God used you as a safe harbor for me during my vulnerable years. I love you!

To all those who have served as spiritual leaders, mentors, and friends in my life: I am thankful for you! I am who I am because God used you to positively shape my life.

FOREWORD

"What a man thinks of himself, that is what determines, or rather indicates, his fate."
—Henry David Thoreau,
American writer & social critic

Thoreau's statement is reminiscent of something Jesus said while He lived among men upon the earth, "Not that which goeth into the mouth defileth a man; but that which cometh out of the mouth, this defileth a man" (Matthew 15:11 KJV). A person's thoughts are some of those things that "goeth out" of him or her and have the capacity to defile. Whether we know it or not, our thoughts help to create our lives. If you do not learn to master your thoughts, you will never gain mastery over your life. If there is something about your life that you are ready to change, begin by changing your thoughts.

You may not realize it, but you have the power to choose your thoughts. No one has the authority to put thoughts into us, because our minds belong to us! It is, therefore, our sacred responsibility and duty to control our thoughts and to be good guardians of them. We have the power to choose the thoughts that will bring us the desired end that we seek. In our thoughts we hold the key to everything that enters our lives.

How we feel and act are predicated upon how we think. Therefore, we need to exercise more care in choosing our thoughts than we do any other thing. The energy in our thoughts affects us greatly, and because of this, we need to be more guided by the Word of God in choosing how we think.

Hand in hand with thoughts is the impact of imaginations over our lives. Imaginations are formulated by the content of our thoughts over time, and they are powerfully crucial to our everyday lives. The imaginations we entertain, good or bad, wage war against our current realities. As Christians, we are called to move from glory to glory (2 Corinthians 3:18). In other words, we should always strive for higher levels in life and destiny, especially in the things of God. But it is impossible to move anywhere, especially to higher levels, without first seeing it in our minds. Our imaginations make us more creative, affording us wings to fly where we once only crawled. Imaginations carry us to worlds that never were, but that can be. We must learn to use them to move us along paths that lead to abundance instead of roads that work against us.

This book is a wholistic biblical treatment of how to effectively deal with our many destructive thoughts and imaginations. Unhelpful thinking and imaginative patterns can have devastating impacts on every area of our lives. But take heart and comfort in this truth: anyone can break free from the grips of these two potential vices. Many people have tried in far too many ways to rid their lives of these potential strongholds once and for all only to discover that, in the long run, their efforts were in vain. This book offers more than short-term strategies to deal with them. It provides readers with insights on how to deal with disruptive thoughts and imaginations from the epicenter of manifestation for the long run, permanently. It offers what I believe is an intelligent and biblical approach to addressing our thinking habits and imaginations, as we transform our situations through the power and application of the tools provided to us in our divine instrument case.

In conclusion, irrespective of the extent to which we have been negatively affected by our thoughts and imaginations, the good news is that with dedicated practice of what this book teaches, we can succeed in replacing them with habits that will truly help to put us over. This can make a huge difference in our day-to-day health, happiness, and comfort. Happy and rewarding reading.

Rev. George Adegboye

INTRODUCTION

Now is the time to break free from the strongholds of self-sabotage and distorted thinking! These intrusive streams of thought are the handiwork of the enemy, and they are responsible for destroying the most critical relationships in your life. *Casting Down Disruptive Imaginations* is an instructional guide for believers who are tired of allowing their negative thoughts to rule their lives.

My personal experience, as well as my years of experience in counseling those who wonder why their life is not producing as it should, inspired me to share this message beyond the pulpit. *Casting Down Disruptive Imaginations* digs beyond the surface level to expose the root causes of this sadly common, cataclysmic condition of living below soaring level.

Before we can effectively cast anything down, there is a preliminary habit we must adopt. We must condition ourselves *never* to allow Satan to interpret situations for us. The only way to keep him from doing this is to know what God has already said concerning situations. Jesus demonstrates for us the most fool-proof way to accomplish this in Matthew 4. At this point in time, Jesus was physically weak from fasting for the past forty days. He was tired and hungry, making Him vulnerable enough for the devil to engage in conversation:

> *The tempter came to him and said, "If you are the Son of God, tell these stones to become bread." Jesus answered, "It is written: 'Man shall not live on bread alone, but on every word that comes from the mouth of God.' Then the devil took him to the holy city and had him stand on the highest point of the temple. "If you are the Son of God," he said, "throw yourself down. For it is written: 'He will command his angels concerning you, and they will lift you up in their hands, so that you will not strike your foot against a stone.'" Jesus answered him, "It is also written: 'Do not put the Lord your God to the test.'" Again, the devil took him to a very high mountain and showed him all the kingdoms of the world and their splendor. "All this I will give you," he said, "If you will bow down and worship me." Jesus said to him, "Away from me, Satan! For it is written: 'Worship the Lord your God and serve him only.'" Then the devil left him, and angels came and attended him.*
>
> **Matthew 4:3-11**

Satan went as far as to tempt Jesus with a shortcut to accomplishing the very thing He was sent to earth to do. If we are not careful, the devil can overwhelm us with anxiety-provoking thoughts concerning our path in life, making his way seem far more palatable. If Jesus did not know God's Word concerning His provisions, His divine protection, and the authority He carried as God's Son, He might have allowed the devil to broker a deal of false exhortation in exchange for suicide.

God knows the end from the beginning, and He desires to share with you everything you need to know for victorious living. He already has systems in place for every situation that will arise. So, we never have to worry or live in dismay. Any thought or imagination that throws you into emotional bondage is a disruption to kingdom-thinking. Any thought or imagination that becomes bigger to you than the Holy Spirit who wills to work through you and for you is disruptive and demonic and must be cast down. Nothing should consume you more than the love of God and the gift of His sweet Holy Spirit.

This book is designed to help you quickly identify and annihilate every negative thought flow and belief system in your life so that you live victoriously. I advise you to keep a notebook, pen, highlighter—and most importantly, your favorite version of the Holy Scriptures—readily available as you read. I have infused this book with the Living Word of God—that is the authority given unto us to recognize and stand against the devil's wiles as you move forward in carrying out God's will for your life. I am a teacher of God's Word, so prepare to be submerged in it. May the Lord empower you for higher living as you read.

IMAGE

SEGMENT ONE

PREVIEW

A ZEBRA'S STRIPES

...He calls his own sheep by name and leads them out. ...and his sheep follow him because they know his voice. But they will never follow a stranger; in fact, they will run away from him because they do not recognize a stranger's voice.
John 10:3b, 4b-5

A few years ago, I came across some interesting information about zebras. Something about the mother zebra captured my attention. The mother zebra is the sole caregiver for her foal. When she has her baby, she retreats from the rest of the herd for several days with her newborn closely at her side. During their time away from the rest of the herd, they bond so intimately that Mommy Zebra is certain her unique stripe pattern is permanently imprinted into the mind of her foal.

As they bond, Baby Zebra comes to distinguish her mom's scent from all other scents, and she acquaints herself to her mommy's voice until it is different from every other voice. If, by chance, Baby Zebra loses her ability to see, she now has more than one way to find her way back to her mother.

The establishment of such a relationship is profound because once it is formed, it becomes virtually unbreakable. The relationship increases the likelihood of the successful development of every other skill the zebra foal must obtain to survive.

Did you know that every zebra has a stripe pattern that is as unique as our human fingerprints? What a meticulous Creator we serve! In a dazzle (herd) of zebras, Baby Zebra can confidently identify the body of stripes most relevant to her well-being. Except at the instruction of Mama Zebra, she will never follow another. It is at this same level that our walk with Christ must begin if we are to withstand Satan's deceit.

* * *

We open this manual with a lesson on *imprinting*, the scientific term used to describe the period when an essential relationship is formed between the care-giving parent and newborn mammal or bird species. Imprinting is not exclusive to natural species alone. As you may have guessed, it holds a spiritual dynamic that is important for us to understand as we prepare to cast down every imagination that has tried to devastate us over the years.

You see, once it became clear to Satan just how God-like mere humans could become, he panicked. In response to his discovery, he waged a war to take place in the most volatile place on earth: our minds. He had already lost the war in heaven. He could only do so much on the earth, given the authority man carried. Only in the minds of human beings does the devil have any chance of winning a battle against our Maker.

In this war, Satan uses simple strategies to lead men astray from God's Word. He has utilized this same strategy since the days of Adam and Eve in the Garden of Eden. All he does is put ideas in our heads—little thoughts, just for us to consider. Without a structure in place to properly interpret and respond to Satan's suggestions, these little thoughts stew around in our subconscious minds until they begin to grow like yeast. These tiny considerations grow into negative, anxiety-based conclusions about our circumstances. Once we choose to fully ingest these conclusions, we end up saying and doing things that rattle our relationships. Here's an example:

ABBY: David hasn't called me all day. His secretary did say he has a full agenda today. Let me watch some TV while I wait.

TV: (*TV narrator*) This week on "CAUGHT UP": (*Brittany*) I can't believe you're cheating on me with Donna, your secretary! Why was I never enough for you?! (*Justin*) Donna, I mean Brittany, I can explain…

DEVIL: Talk about reality television! I wonder why it took Brittany so long to figure out that Justin was cheating on her. All the signs of infidelity were there…

DISRUPTION: I'm sure it's no big deal. It's not the first time David has been late. He probably didn't call because he's doing something very important, more important than calling me. Donna, or whatever his secretary's name is, might be there late as well. I wonder what she looks like… Maybe I should call his office again… That skinny secretary better not answer his phone! (Though it is her job to answer it!)

Imagine. An image from the television planted itself in Abby's mind until she envisioned herself having the same experience as a fictional character! That one mental picture could result in a string of silently hostile evenings, when they could have been using the time to enjoy each other's company in the presence of God. Disruptive imaginations have a way of creating untimely isolation. Imagine what they could have used that time to birth if not for the satanic interruption.

Now, do you understand why ungodly imaginations must be shut down and cast out immediately? Satan employs the most subtle suggestions to distract us. We cannot be subtle in our response. If nothing is done concerning Abby's faulty thought pattern, she will remain exposed to more heightened versions of disruption, and it will not take long before what she is imagining begins to find expression in her everyday activity.

* * *

We live in a time where fantasy is glorified. From scary movies and emotionally charged dramas to the anxious anticipation of Santa Claus or the Tooth Fairy. We are conditioned, from childhood, to engage real life with the realities we've imagined for ourselves. The disappointment we encountered when we learned there was no Tooth Fairy or Santa Claus was real! The fear of the dark we developed after letting our minds dwell on many scary movies has real consequences. Our minds become trained to accept the dictates of our irrational thoughts and emotions.

This book equips the children of God to cast down every imagination disrupting the advancement of God's kingdom in their lives and on earth. God has made available to us everything we need to withstand the wiles of Satan. No longer will our faulty thinking lead us down paths of destruction. No longer will we be consumed with the heavy burdens of anxiety, fear, and depression. Those burdens are gifts from the father of lies himself, purposed to deter and distract us from building the bonds that will ultimately destroy him. The burdens keep us from perfect harmony with God, our Father, through Christ Jesus.

In this segment, entitled "Image," get ready to learn about God's pre-designed templates for living victoriously. Once you are familiar with the original templates, prepare to learn how to quickly identify and dismiss the imitation images the devil will use to keep you in bondage. Today, the distorted images Satan has been using to imprint his authority over your mind are broken permanently, in Jesus Christ's name!

CHAPTER ONE

THE IMPRINTING PHENOMENON

Can a mother forget the baby at her breast and have no compassion on the child she has borne? Though she may forget, I will not forget you! See, I have engraved you on the palms of my hands; your walls are ever before me.

Isaiah 49:15-16

The word *imprint* is most commonly received as zoological jargon, referencing the natural attachment patterns of nurturers and their offspring as a basis for the transferal of survival skills. *Imprinting* also describes the state of an item becoming indefinitely fixed on a specific platform, much like a tattoo on a person's arm. Still in other cases, "to imprint" is synonymous with "to stamp," "to emboss," "to inscribe," or "to engrave."[1] In every case, *imprinting* leaves a long, if not everlasting, impression on its subject that is significant enough to alter its appearance, function, and value forever.

When I explained the zebra's imprinting process to you earlier on, I mentioned sight, scent, and sound as senses critical to the effectiveness of bond development. Physical touch and taste are also essential components of the imprinting process. Once a foal has tasted her mother's milk, no other sustenance compares. She doesn't know that her mother's milk has every nutrient her body needs to strengthen her immune system, or that the milk is formulated specifically with her digestive and other physiological needs in mind. She just knows it's the best she ever had, and that no other fluid compares.

As the mare leads her foal on their imprinting excursion, the two remain so close, they are almost physically inseparable. The average foal learns to walk rather quickly and could stray away or linger behind if she so desired. Instead, she abides safely at mom's side, making skin-to-skin contact as often as she can. The physical touch that takes place between mare and foal is not a product of fear for either party, in most cases. Baby Zebra is not leaning on mom to keep from falling once she has her stride. Mama Zebra can keep her child safe standing a foot or two away.

The physical touch between the two is best described as love-based. Mom's constant touch is a lasting reminder for Baby Zebra that she is ever present with warmth, wisdom, and provision to keep her safe during her formative years. Baby's nuzzling and constant leaning on mom indicates attunement to their time together. Baby is learning, which means mom can continue stepping up the lessons.

God designed a comparable system for our well-being. We call it fellowship, or communion. The purpose of this time is to enhance our attunement to His voice, will, and way. God's first reveal of the imprinting period can be seen in the Garden of Eden as He walked and talked with Adam daily. Study Genesis chapters 1 through 3 [2]and you will see, verse by verse, how God desired to establish an unbreakable covenant with Adam. The more time they spent together, the more Adam would come into full knowledge of his identity as a son of God.

God made sure Adam knew His voice the moment he was created (Genesis 1:28-29). God's voice was distinguishable from any other sound, because it always came with a proclamation of provision, instruction, and valuable information. God ensured that Adam knew the depth and power of His love by way of His mighty hands. He spoke universes into existence, but for the creation made in His image, He designed and provided for him by His righteous hand. He did this for no other creation.

Whenever God did something great for Adam like providing him with the capacity for eternal life,[3] with a residence in total paradise,[4] or with a mate that would suit him perfectly for the rest of his life on earth,[5] He did so manually, so Adam could feel the intimate, meticulous care He had for him.

As He spoke with Adam, He showed him the pattern of His design and how all things worked together for him. God did these things so that Adam could know Him as God, the creator and sustainer of life, and so that he might know just how much authority he was designed to carry. To date, God establishes points in time for us to learn His voice and His way through the gift of His Son, Jesus Christ, and by way of our Comforter, the Holy Spirit. He desires that we taste and see that He is good[6] and that we are made in His image.

What Satan aspires to do is to get us to the point where God 's voice and will are unrecognizable to us. If He can get us to think in a way contrary to God's heart, it is only a matter of time before our actions become misaligned. So, he implements his version of the imprinting season, where he identifies every opportunity on earth to expose you to his voice—or better, your own voice. Once you know the voice of God, you can't really confuse it again. But if he can catch you out of God's presence at any time, he can make enough suggestions to deceive you into allowing a strange voice to become a voice familiar enough for you to follow into folly.

The Bible references Satan as the father of lies. See how Jesus describes him in John 8:44 as He rebukes the Pharisees. By then, the devil had successfully taken most of the religious leaders through his imprinting process:

> *You belong to your father, the devil, and you*
> *want to carry out your father's desires. He was*
> *a murderer from the beginning, not holding to*
> *the truth, for there is no truth in him. When he*
> *lies, he speaks his native language, for he is a*
> *liar and the father of lies.*

John 8:44

The devil is a liar! It is completely true. But he is not a liar to those who belong to Christ Jesus. In fact, the devil won't lie to anyone who has had close encounters with God, such as Adam and Eve in the Garden of Eden. If a person has never known the truth, they will believe anything. Satan can lie to them and it will become their reality.

For those of us who know Christ Jesus, we won't fall for the falsities. Even if we might, we are backed with the gift of the Holy Spirit to help us discern. We have angels assigned to protect us and fight for us. Jesus intercedes for us. God, Himself, will even step in to intervene if the situation requires. But alas, we are human with free will, and the Lord will never impose His help on us. So, if we choose for a moment to put our guard down and step out of God's presence purely for exploratory reasons, there is room for the "accuser of the brethren" to challenge us to rethink everything we thought we knew.

Yes, to the world, the devil is a liar. To the believer, he is a deceiver. A little deception goes a long way in triggering our entertainment of counterproductive thoughts and images. Once such images are formed, they linger until they are challenged and shut down. If they are not shut down, they will linger and grow as imaginations, until they become full-fledged strongholds.

Once a stronghold is formed, it can only be broken by the blood and wonder-working Word of Jesus Christ. Every action and decision you make before receiving deliverance through Christ Jesus is enslavement. Strongholds envelope you, smother every destiny-relevant relationship. They consume your senses until you can hardly see or hear anyone else, including the Holy Spirit. If you do manage to hear the still, small voice longing to bring you back to reality, you hardly believe it, because the devil has already successfully imprinted his images into your mind and fortified them.

By the time you do manage to hear the voice of reason and truth and try to break free of it, the stronghold has already established a pattern in your life. It will be as if you have become addicted to poverty, anxiety, self-pity, worry, or whatever else he has convinced you to believe! He will then bind you to the trap of lies you fell into. How do we keep from falling prey to such deceit? Compare God's first dialogue with man to Satan's. What is the difference?

Dialogue with God

- **Genesis 1:28:** God communicates blessings of increase and authority. He provides explicit instruction.
- **Genesis 1:29-30:** God explains to Adam that the purpose of His gift of all seed and fruit-bearing plants is for his consumption and to feed all of creation.
- **Genesis 2:16:** God communicates to Adam a clear directive and its consequence after sharing with him the benefits and boundaries of his liberty in the garden.
- **Genesis 2:18:** God shares concern and His action steps to address His observation of Adam's state as it relates to his destiny.
- **OUTCOME**: Upon receipt of God's gift and instruction, Adam expressed his understanding of what the Lord had said and done as he excercised his authority to name and commission his destiny helper.

Dialogue with Satan

- **Genesis 3:1b:** Satan questions God's instructions to the woman, adding extremity to the original limit given.
- **Genesis 3:2-3:** She replies to Satan with a mildly exaggerated recount of God's warning and instruction.
- **Genesis 3:4-5:** Satan tells her she "...will not *certainly* die.." causing her to consider the possibility of another outcome and to imagine what it might be like to eat the forbidden fruit.
- **OUTCOME**: Her imagined experience became the sole catalyst for her reasoning and decision-making. The resultant "opened eyes" gave way to the humans' first encounter with fear (emotive state driven by imagined possibilities of harm or danger). Fear drove a series of poor decisions in response to their disobedience, all resulting in eternal consequences.

THE FORCE OF RELATIONSHIP

There are two ways you must never treat relationships: equally or casually. There is a biblical report of God's resolve immediately after eyeballing Adam, His treasured creation, in the Garden of Eden, asserting, "It is not good for man to be alone." Here God establishes for us that for anything to be productive, it must partner with someone. Your relationships matter. When you study Genesis 2 mentioned above, you learn that God considered every other animal and decided that none of them were a suitable mate for Adam[7]. Consider some of the most essential aspects of our faith:

- God is One, personified as God the Father, Son, and Holy Spirit.
- Holy matrimony between one man and one woman, becoming as one flesh and empowered to fruitfulness.
- The divinely orchestrated body of Christ as one body with many parts.

What do all these definitions have in common? They're communicating a message. God demonstrates that anything of eternal value requires the collaborative efforts of God on earth, a system whereby everyone has his divine assignment, and no man's assignment can be fully completed in isolation.

> *Though one may be overpowered, two can defend themselves. A cord of three strands is not quickly broken.*
> **Ecclesiastes 4:12**

Both the relationships you form, as well as the important relationships you choose not to invest in, aid in determining your level of vulnerability with such mediums. Every Christian should have a destiny team comprised of a person or people who help keep you grounded and focused, reducing your risks of being swept away by the cares of this life.

God gave me all sorts of people who imprinted lasting impressions in my heart and mind. They imprinted positive images of divinely orchestrated experiences, filling me up with the truth that I am fearfully and wonderfully made and valuable to God.

I was seventeen when I established a relationship with my spiritual parents in the Lord. This relationship came right on time! I managed to graduate high school successfully, despite the challenges I faced through my parents' divorce. As bold as I was in my pursuit of higher education, I was still filled with many insecurities and uncertainties about my place in the world. If I had not had an encounter with God through the provision of my spiritual parents, I probably would have landed in the ditch! They were a safe harbor for me.

God knew exactly what I needed at the time, and He blessed me with my spiritual father and mother two weeks into my university experience. They were eagles, and took me under their spiritual wings as one of their own. Their teaching and counsel edified me so much that my passion for the things of God intensified exponentially. They also provided a safe space in their home where I could come, spend hours, and just be…there was no judgment, but love and acceptance. I would go to their home first thing in the morning, relax, laugh, love, and be loved in a godly environment. I worshipped the Lord freely, for as long as my heart desired. When I was on my college breaks, I would race over to their home and play Ron Kenoly's musical video "Lift Him Up" and would dance for hours. To date, it is still one of my favorite worship DVDs. It is nostalgic for me and places my heart in a state of gratitude.

My spiritual parents weren't the only relationships I acquired that made a significant difference in my life. I had been exposed to so much pain as a result of coming from a broken home. I was insecure. I felt sorry for myself. I lacked confidence. I was fearful. Many unscriptural images had formed in my mind, based on the spirit-crushing things I encountered over time. The Lord knew the risks that lay ahead and how I could have easily fallen into the wrong hands. But in the most vulnerable moments of my life, God made sure there were godly people divinely placed in my life, to keep me on track for His will for me.

As a little girl in Michigan, when my parents were fighting and having troubles, God gave me a kind neighbor. She was a lady who had been hired to teach me how to play the piano. After school, I would either go to her apartment or play from our apartment for hours and hours! Against the noise, she taught me that I could still make beautiful music. I can't play it very well anymore. But because of her, I learned to play when I needed to the most.

Do you see? My relationship with God produced in me a strong recognition of His glorious presence through the people of God whom He sent my way. Like Baby Zebra to Mommy Zebra, I cleaved to God very early in age. No matter what deception Satan threw my way, I could never sustain a belief that I was unwanted or unloved for long, because I could recognize His voice, His touch, and His sacrificial stripes in the people He appointed to minister into my life.

Righteous relationships keep you safe. When you surround yourself with the people of God, you limit opportunities for Satan to distract you with demonically-inspired imaginations. It starts with your decision to acknowledge

Jesus Christ as Lord and Savior of your life. From there, His passionate commitment towards you takes over. It will amaze you what structures and functions He puts in place to assure you that He has never left you, and He will never forsake you.

CASE STUDY

In Isaiah 49:15-16, God expresses the permanency of His passionate commitment towards the people of Israel through Prophet Isaiah during very tumultuous times. For decades, the Israelites had been warned by judges and prophets. Their constant refusal to trust in the God of their forefathers over pagan gods would trigger the judgment of the Almighty God. That was finally being executed, and as a result, they were exiled from their homeland and scattered about like seeds in a foreign land. All the while, the best of their land was being distributed to the citizens of their conquerors, the Babylonians, while they found themselves in the same enslaved state God had first delivered them from.

The Israelites' spirits had sunken to an all-time low, encumbered with fear, guilt, and hopelessness as a result of all they had suffered, first by the Assyrians and now the Babylonians. See how they grieved:

> *But Zion said, "The Lord has forsaken me, the Lord has forgotten me."*
>
> **Isaiah 49:14**

But God responded to their cry, as He always did, with this rebuttal:

> *"Can a mother forget the baby at her breast and have no compassion on the child she has borne? Though she may forget, I will not forget you! See, I have engraved you on the palms of my hands; your walls are ever before me. Your children hasten back, those who laid you waste depart from you. Lift up your eyes and look around; all your children gather and come to you. As surely as I live," declares the Lord, "you will wear them all as ornaments; you will put them on, like a bride."*
> **Isaiah 49:15-18**

Another translation puts it this way:

> *See, I have tattooed your name upon my palm, and ever before me is a picture of Jerusalem's walls in ruins.*
> **Isaiah 49:16 (TLB)**

God's desire for His children to put their trust in Him, the One who divinely orchestrated their freedom and met their every need, never died—though their love for Him fizzled at every opportunity.

COVENANT RELATIONSHIP

There is nothing like basking in the presence of God… hearing His voice…and resting in His promises! I remember how it was when I first came into full fellowship with God as a young child. You learn, as you spend time with Him, that He always gives you what you need, when you need it. At the time I needed it most, God gave me spiritual parents. They would allow me to come into their home and worship for hours on end, uninterrupted, in their living room. I remember, loosely, that guests would stop by and my spiritual father would inform them, "She is dancing before her Father. She has taken over the TV." I was spoiled by them. That is what I needed for that period of my life. Time to be healed and loved, and to develop my intimacy with the Lord, without negative thoughts or the cares of this world interrupting my time with the Father. When you know God intimately, you cannot be deceived by imaginations.

The promises of God are sure. One thing you must be clear about is the truth that you have already won. From the days of our exodus from Eden to the days of the cross, and even up to now, Satan has demonstrated his mission to keep us out of relationship with God so that we end up falling into a pit of self-righteousness or hopelessness. He knows that if he can keep us from God's presence, he can keep us from the truth—that we already have our victory in Christ Jesus. But if we remain ambivalent about our destiny we will go on, easily distracted by deceptive imaginations, fighting the wrong battles, or failing to fight at all to defend our victory that is in Christ Jesus.

YOUR IMPRINTER

I once witnessed a man who happened to have extremely high blood pressure being fed a meal while he was sitting in his bedroom. They made him rest and do absolutely nothing.

Still, they couldn't get his blood pressure down. After several months, he eventually died.

I saw this when I was about nine years old. About the same year, I became aware of a family friend who was having an extramarital affair. I also witnessed the stress on the face of a church member who had lost her job and was struggling to find another one while she attempted to make ends meet for her family. I witnessed Christians who would fight all the way into the church, and then they would slap on their church face, smile, and dance throughout the service. It was astonishing!

All these images stuck with me for a very long time and played a critical role in my attitude and how I made decisions. Eventually, I began to understand that this is Satan's prime strategy for his war against Christians. He wants to imprint upon our spirit man so that we never get into right standing with God—and if we do get there, he wants to be sure that we can't stay there.

TRAUMA

Post-traumatic stress disorder (PTSD) is another name for the residual effect of negative imprinting on your soul or brain. This kind of imprinting can take place when we experience what we call trauma. Trauma takes place when you experience something that your spirit is unequipped to handle. When you are met, unprepared, with an issue of life, a door of disruption opens, causing delay or impeding your ability to develop certain skills or functions. To date, 44.7 million Americans have been diagnosed with PTSD. This doesn't include the countless individuals who go undiagnosed.[8] Those who don't identify and address the symptoms of trauma within the first three months hardly ever recover. Secondary traumatic stress mimics PTSD. But spiritually, symptoms of PTSD can be removed. So, though it's imprinted, it doesn't mean it's imprinted permanently. It just means it is there. Now, you must get rid of it! The worst thing is…you don't have to experience it to live it. Let's take a moment to study John 10:7-11.

> *Therefore Jesus said again, "Very truly I tell you, I am the gate for the sheep. All who have come before me are thieves and robbers, but the sheep have not listened to them. I am the gate; whoever enters through me will be saved. They will come in and go out, and find pasture. The thief comes only to steal and kill and destroy; I have come that they may have life, and have it to the full. I am the good shepherd. The good shepherd lays down his life for the sheep."*
> **John 10:7-11**

When you take in anything through your natural senses (especially without context), one of two interpreters will provide you with information about your experience. Each interpreter has a very specific platform by which to educate you. Satan will give you the facts. He will engage your experience or level of understanding to tell you how things look.

The Holy Spirit will give you the truth. He will engage the wisdom of the Ancient of Days, prophecies (spoken or written) that have gone forth ahead of time concerning you or the situation at hand. He will use the covenant promises of God, His infallible Word, and His track record to tell you what you have just seen or experienced. You must decide which will be your reality.

The information that you take in, once interpreted, will take one of two routes. Both routes will pitstop at the mind. One route allows the information received to linger in your mind a little longer and to mix with other pieces of information or ideas before moving you to action.

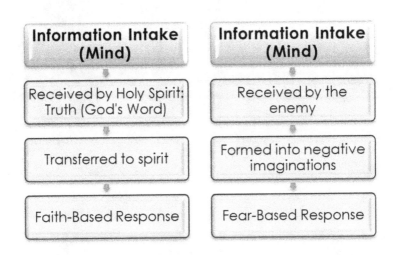

CHAPTER TWO

THE DANGERS OF IMAGINATION

And God saw that the wickedness of man was great in the earth, and that every imagination of the thoughts of his heart was only evil continually.

Genesis 6:5 (KJV)

Like so many people, I come from a broken home. I did not understand it at the time, but when your family system has been damaged, every member of the family suffers from the trauma of your home dismantling. The brokenness spreads like a cancer, and it's not uncommon for that hurt to transcend generations.

When I was almost ten years old, I recall an older family member looking at me with disgust and disapproval. I was baffled, yet not surprised. I was getting used to being verbally and emotionally abused. "You have the eyes of a thief," he scoffed. The hatred in his eyes burned into my soul. I was very confused. I stared in the mirror for hours. What did he see? What did he know that I didn't know? Was I going to end up in jail? Was I going to become a serial killer? What was I going to become in the future?

That judgment stuck with me for quite some time. I internalized it. I questioned my self-worth and judgment. Was I born a bad person, full of envy and evil? What was it about me that would make someone say such a thing to a child? *Maybe it's true; I must be a naturally bad person... I can't be trusted*, I recall thinking to myself.

At that time, I didn't understand that when people who were once in love have children, then have discord, there is the likelihood that they will take their frustrations and resentment out on the offspring, because they see the person they now resent in them. The same goes for many other situations. When people are unable to channel their feelings appropriately, they will find someone to project their resentment onto. That someone might be you, though their frustrations truly have nothing to do with you. What that family member said to me was a negative prophecy spoken over my life that I had to learn to reject and cast down.

I had to learn to stand in front of a mirror and say what God's Word says about me: I am the righteousness of God in Christ Jesus! I am the apple of God's eye! I am tattooed on the palm of His hand! Before I was conceived in my mother's womb, He knew me, He called me, and He chose me.[1] God designed me in His image, and every thought and plan He predestined regarding me is great! It is not possible for me to have the eyes of a thief. I am made in my Father's image. I have eyes as sharp and insightful as an eagle's eye!

My parents divorced when I was a little girl. My siblings and I were taken away from our mother. A lot of negative things were spoken over us that the Lord had to deliver me from, because those words stirred up imaginations that led to

---

[1] 2 Corinthians 5:21 | Deut. 32:10 | Isaiah 49: 16 | Jeremiah 1:5

a faulty belief system. When people around you are broken, they begin to tear down everyone around them. This is especially so in family settings where situations such as abuse and divorce have taken place.

THE POWER OF IMAGINATION

When you imagine something, you allow your mind to gather bits of images collected over time to form new images and sensations. Though you have never experienced these images physically, everything you have ever imagined is based on your exposure to natural experiences. Now, the imaginations that you form and allow to regularly saturate your thoughts dictate what comes to fruition regarding your beliefs and actions.

An imagination is something you can just sit down and dream of. The devil loves it when we just sit and dream most of the time. He loves it when you watch the news, because you will likely see something that bothers your emotions. You might dream about it or obsess over it, until suddenly, you are dreaming of it and it becomes your reality, even though it never happened to you.

Have you ever found yourself praying, hoping, and working assiduously for something good to happen concerning you or a loved one, when out of nowhere, an image of something that is sure to ruin your good outcome begins to materialize? Did the image consume your thoughts and manipulate every factor involved in your affair? Let me paint you a picture:

You know a good marriage when you see one. Your newsfeeds are flooded with their wedding stories. You grew up watching happily married couples hugged up and holding hands in various places. And every Sunday you know you'll be met with one testimony or the other from the "Johnsons," the church power couple. You have these images of marriage, at its best, etched into the various awnings in your mind. Every picture is familiar and nostalgic.

You have also seen a marriage, meant to last forever, dissolve before your young eyes. Now, there's a series of murals splattered elaborately in your mental gallery, displaying every sight, scent, sound, and sentiment you sustained as you learned how suddenly and sourly marriages could end.

Those sour images faded far into the recesses of your mind as you grew older and found the true love of your life. You finally say, "I do," and as soon as you do, a renaissance takes place, resurrecting those murals you'd forgotten about.

Over the course of time and experiences, images resurface, each one in correspondence to your efforts to have the best marriage ever. Your images are so overwhelming now that you can almost touch them. Your life is greying, but those murals and awnings are large and vibrant like life itself, or like life should have been. At this point, it only makes sense to embrace them as such. After all, images are all you can see.

You don't recall how or when, but the day came when you accepted the images as a collective and crowned it as your destiny. Maybe you don't recall this either, but the day you exalted the images was the day you acquiesced into a state of unfulfillment.

All the footage in your mind confirms that there is nothing you can do to keep your marriage from shattering before you ever see your twelve-year anniversary. Why did you ever think you could sustain a marriage, when your mother and father could not sustain theirs? Didn't you learn from the Johnsons at church? Only couples who can afford to travel for exotic vacations can have a beautiful marriage. Didn't your aunt tell you that if you couldn't improve your skills in the kitchen or bedroom, you would never be woman enough to keep his interest? How foolish you are to think you had what it took to keep her interest until death did you part, when you can't even keep a job. In fact, maybe death should come earlier. Maybe it's time to part from this life altogether...

Does this scenario sound like anything you have ever experienced? As diligently as you work to make things right, you find yourself exerting unsurmountable effort to prevent what seems inevitable, and it all fails anyway. After that, you are met with splintering thoughts of self-pity and despair as you are forced to accept and mentally recite what clearly are the facts: *This is just how life is for me. I will never be good enough.* I know I am not the only one who has experienced this!

Such feelings and experiences are not uncommon! They are, however, indicative of the impressions you allowed your mind to form concerning specific events. These impressions become the information that shapes your belief system. If you are a Christian and you are weighed down with the cares of this world, the truth is that you made a choice to exalt an image of yourself and your situation above God and His design for your life. Whose image of you and your affairs is most accurate—yours, or that of the One who cared meticulously enough to distinguish every hair and fingerprint in the world to reflect His infinite ability?

DESTINY DICTATORS

Despite the brokenness experienced in my home, I used to pray that my parents wouldn't die young. I prayed this prayer regularly, because I had witnessed the tragedy that happened to two families when the breadwinner died (without life insurance). The kids were shipped off to relatives who, in turn, used them as domestic help (modern day slavery). My prayers were fear-based. I preferred the nightmare that I was experiencing rather than the thought of having to deal with anything worse! I was petrified that things would continue to go from bad, to worse, to worst! While prayer is good, there are some things you need not give your attention. This includes the devil's lies. Don't forget that the devil is a liar, but to the believer, he is a deceiver. Don't let Satan dish out anxiety and wrong confessions disguised as prayer points to you.

If you want to live in accordance with the life God has designed for you, all you must do is live by the dictates of His kingdom. If you don't live conscious of the Lord God's dictates, by default, you will live by and die by Satan's lies. Let's look at some of these dictators:

Your Tongue

There is power in your tongue. Just as God framed our entire world by His words, you have the power to frame your life by the words you speak. When you are faced with strange or challenging situations, how do you respond? Do you sit quietly and allow your thoughts to take over? Do you allow the situation to dictate your entire future? Do you say what you feel? If your answer is yes to any of these, then you are living beneath your privilege. One privilege you have as a child of God is the grace to speak over situations. Don't speak according to feelings or circumstances. Speak according to faith and the promises established in the Word of God.

Exposure

Imaginations are a creative wonder. With your imagination, anything is possible. However, your mind cannot invent images. Imaginations consist only of what we have exposed ourselves to over time. When you expose your mind to destructive things, you give room for negative imaginations to form. Be mindful of what you allow yourself to watch. Be mindful of what you listen to. It will eventually shape your thought flow and actions.

CHAPTER THREE

THE POINT OF ORIGIN

So God created man in his own image; in the
image of God He created him; male and female
He created them.
Genesis 1:27 (NKJV)

I n this chapter, we observe the value of the original.
There's a blueprint that gives a standard to everything
worth copying. Have you taken the time to truly know
your source? Who or what serves as the blueprint for your
life? Where did your value system come from? If you desire
to be successful in life, this is a question you must be able to
proffer an answer to.

The devil knows your Source, and he has made it his
priority to keep you in ignorance. Why? He cannot afford to
risk you obtaining or retaining your Source's values or operating system. If you and too many others begin to perfectly
imitate your Source of origin, everyone on earth will see the
benefits, receive revelation, and be drawn to take on the same
glorious image, leaving Satan without a leg to stand on.[2]

---

[2] John 12:32

THE ORIGINAL IMAGE

At the root of every *imagination* is an *image*. Let's look at the definition of *image*, as we prepare to better understand *imaginations* and why the exalted ones must be cast down:

> **Im·age** *(noun): a representation of the external form of a person or thing in art. The general impression that you are soaring; everything you see appears so much smaller in comparison to the road set before you.*
>
> *(Merriam-Webster)*

Picture an eagle majestically gliding over the affairs of this life, focused, and perfectly in sync with the wind upon which its wings glide. Now, think about wielding the power to cast down imaginations and everything that desires to keep you in bondage. When you have a bird's-eye view, the task of taking down strongholds is far less daunting. Why? You can see the bigger picture! When you are soaring as God designed you to, you will see everything from the point of glorious advantage!

The first images on earth were designed to reflect the kingdom, power, and glory of God so that every being, natural and spirit alike, will recognize the power of His majesty. Human beings were designed first to develop, then to reflect the reality of a divine, fruitful relationship between God the Father, Son, and Holy Spirit.

If you want to cast down disruptive imaginations, you will need to accept this statement as truth. Once you receive a revelation of God through Christ Jesus, your identity, capacity, and the authority you carry become clearer. You will have a better sense of purpose. When this happens, you will not want to remain passive about the negative thoughts and images that trouble you. In fact, you will begin to see them not only as problematic, but as an enemy of your destiny.

The Image of God

God sees the end before the beginning. He is Alpha and Omega. In other words, there is nothing that can happen on this side of eternity that He did not foresee and plan for before it occurs. This includes the presence of sin on the earth, the very force designed to keep you out of God's presence and out of His will. Before man ever sinned, God's Son was destined to eradicate sin and its consequences from our lives—permanently—should we choose to accept Him and His precious gift of salvation.

God knew creating you came with serious challenges. But He also knew you were worth it. You were created in His image so that sin, a governing force on the earth, would have no power over you; neither would death, nor its consequence. God created you in His image, affording you dominion, the power of creation, the power of choice, and the power to speak. All these are needed to overcome Satan's deceit, so all mankind can witness the power, the love, and the glory made available to those who choose to accept His kingship over their lives.

YOUR DESIGN

I have come to understand that it is by God's Word that we can soar in all circumstances. You were never designed to be limited in this life. There is nothing on earth or in the spirit realm that God has not equipped you to rise above and conquer (except Himself). So many of us have allowed our wings to be clipped. We have allowed our destinies to get just beyond our reach, because we did not take the time to come into the full knowledge of our divine make-up and Maker. If we did, we would never fall prey to a disposition of defeat.

How does this happen? Sadly, the devil knows more about our glorious image than we do. He knows you were meant to fly high. Satan wants you to occupy your time with struggle, apprehension, and hopelessness, so that you never arrive in time to make an impact. His best option is to ensure that we never know how high we can fly. He uses our imaginations to distract and deter us from making strides in life.

You can't soar like an eagle if you have weights on! You could be the eagle who flies highest amongst eagles. But if your legs are weighed down and your wings are clipped, you can never soar. Even if you do manage to glide some, you can't achieve your optimal height. In the name of Jesus Christ, as you read this book, those weights will be permanently broken!

RELATIONSHIP

Our relationship with God must be one of Father to child. If we do not see our relationship this way, then we will not receive all the benefits that being a son/daughter in the kingdom of God has to offer. By original design, imprinting is a process meant to take place between the parent and child. If one does not assume the position of "son" or "daughter," the imprinting process can become distorted and, without knowing it, a person can begin to take on the characteristics and point of view of an entity that does not have a Father's heart towards them, creating all manner of confusion in the long run.

Case Study

In the book of Joshua, chapter 14, Caleb shares an account of how he came to understand the dynamic personality of God:

> *I was forty years old when Moses the servant of the Lord sent me from Kadesh Barnea to explore the land. And I brought him back a report according to my convictions, but my fellow Israelites who went up with me made the hearts of the people melt in fear. I, however, followed the Lord my God wholeheartedly. So on that day Moses swore to me, "The land on which your feet have walked will be your inheritance and that of your children forever, because you have followed the Lord my God wholeheartedly." Now then, just as the Lord promised, he has kept me alive for forty-five years since the time he said this to Moses, while Israel moved about in the wilderness. So here I am today, eighty-five years old! I am still as strong today as the day Moses sent me out; I'm just as vigorous to go out to battle now as I was then. Now give me this hill country that the Lord promised me that day. You yourself heard then that the Anakites were there and their cities were large and fortified, but, the Lord helping me, I will drive them out just as he said.*
>
> **Joshua 14:7-12**

You cannot even begin to understand God properly when you are not in a covenant relationship with Him. As much as He is unchanging, He is multi-breasted. He longs to show us, in detail, all the wonders of His ways through relationship. When you develop a relationship with God, you get to know Him more, and it changes your perceptions.

The first step in establishing your relationship with the Lord is to come into the knowledge of who He is on your behalf. Caleb gives us the account of his fellow Israelites' trip to survey the land in Kadesh Barnea. They gave a dreadful report to the people, because that is what they saw and understood. But Caleb, who was sent to survey the same land, at the same time, had a very different report—not because he was blindly optimistic or saw something totally different, but rather, he had a better understanding of God and saw things according to the promise God had given. As you read Caleb's report, you learn that over time, Caleb got to know God as One who keeps His promises and One who is mighty in battle, always ready to help His children in the time of war.

When Caleb saw the Anakites in the land, it was from a bird's-eye view. He went, soaring, to carry out the assignment given him. As he saw the Anakites, he also saw the land God had promised him, and he saw that the Anakites were not too big for His God to evict. On the other hand, his fellow surveyors could not see past their emotions. Their vision was limited to what they could see, and what they had come to understand over time about the inhabitants of the land and their stature. To date, most people form conclusions based on natural experiences. They don't know how limited their five senses are, until it's too late. The Bible tells us in Proverbs:

> *Trust in the Lord with all your heart and lean not on your own understanding; in all your ways submit to him, and he will make your paths straight.*
> **Proverbs 3:5-6**

Like Caleb, the other Israelites who surveyed the land had experienced God at work before, and victory had been accomplished. They knew His hand. From the parting of the Red Sea to the sweet taste of the miracle of manna that fell from the sky in a time of drought and famine, they had tasted and seen God's goodness in the gloomiest of circumstances. Why, then, were they not able to see this situation of the land's inhabitants from the same perspective as Caleb and Joshua? The Israelites were so close to the promise, but they could not even envision victory as an option. Their imaginations ran wild with the countless ways in which they might be destroyed.

> Then Caleb silenced the people before Moses and said, "We should go up and take possession of the land, for we can certainly do it." But the men who had gone up with him said, "We can't attack those people; they are stronger than we are." And they spread among the Israelites a bad report about the land they had explored. They said, "The land we explored devours those living in it. All the people we saw there are of great size. We saw the Nephilim there (the descendants of Anak come from the Nephilim). We seemed like grasshoppers in our own eyes, and we looked the same to them."
> **Numbers 13:30-33**

What distinguished Joshua and Caleb's testimony from that of their counterparts? *Relationship.* Caleb and Joshua remained in fellowship with the Lord. Their imaginations ran just as wild, but differently! Their imagination was based on their image of God, their Father, whose heart beat for them. They knew Him by His heart. They were His sons.

Chosen, loved, protected, and provided for by their Father. It is the heart of the Father that you will accept Him as such, knowing fully well that you are His child, His chosen one, with whom you desire to abide forever.

There are so many people carrying the weight of their past with them daily. People walk around for years carrying burdens such as despair, loneliness, and hopelessness. Such people believe that no one cares for them, or that because of whatever circumstance or experience, they are unworthy of true love. So many people come from broken homes, and as a result, they walk around with broken hearts, shattered by the words and actions of those they once held deeply in their hearts. Establishing your relationship with Christ is more important than any other relationship you are trying to hold on to. It sets the tone for how you will engage with others.

Friends, we cannot afford to waste time feeling sorry for ourselves. We must live with the consciousness that we have a time-sensitive purpose to fulfill. There are some things that we do not have time for, because they are time-wasters. The disruptive, destructive, and demonic imaginations that exalt themselves above God's Word for our lives are some of them. Once we are born again, God equips us with all we need to accomplish His will on the earth.

Until you know God, you will never know who you truly are. We have talked about how God designed you to soar. That's just the foundation. You were made in God's image. Just as we described Him as multi-breasted, you too have so many traits and gifts in addition to the anointing you were meant to carry. But if you do not know who you are in totality, you are easy prey for the devil to assign a fake identity to. He does not want you to know how much authority you carry, or what weapons you can access to combat his evil plans concerning you.

THE IMPOSTER

> *The god of this age has blinded the minds of unbelievers, so that they cannot see the light of the gospel that displays the glory of Christ, who is the image of God.*
>
> **2 Corinthians 4:4**

At a tender age, we are introduced to very graphic images that we will remember for the rest of our lives. These images are the introduction to Satan's plan for dictating the destruction of our destinies. If you are a Christian parent, don't wait too long to teach your children these three things: who their God is, who they are, and who the devil is. Many of us don't really know how the devil operates. We have this image of him that has been distorted by media and stories of fantasy.

A Deceiver

We all know that the devil is a liar. According to God's Word, he is the father of lies.[9] In the case of the nonbeliever, this is true. He uses lies to keep people in the dark to rob them of their victory. But Christians have access to the truth, making it difficult for Satan to use lies as his weapon of choice. So, the devil is a liar, but to the Christian believer he's not just a liar but a great deceiver. He gives Christians partial truths and distorted interpretations of events, and he drops superfluous facts in place of the truth God originally gave you. Satan's goal is to imprint his version of reality on your mind to rob you of truth. Coach Satan wants to condition you to fail at the game of life.

Maybe you witnessed the impact of the death of a loved one at a very early age. Perhaps you experienced trauma after witnessing the devastations of divorce. Did you witness life as the child of an alcoholic or a drug addict? Did you see poverty…neglect? Were you forced to see the face of someone who abused or molested you throughout your childhood on a regular basis?

When you experience such things, the various images of what you witnessed find a way of returning to you. You can be watching a movie, and suddenly it all comes back. The images haunt you for days, until you are back in the room you were in when you were twelve, or eight, or even five years old. This is how the devil imprints. Today, the Lord will permanently pull down those images, in Jesus Christ's name.

CHAPTER FOUR

THE POINT OF REVELATION

I pray that the eyes of your heart may be enlightened in order that you may know the hope to which he has called you, the riches of his glorious inheritance in his holy people, and his incomparably great power for us who believe.
Ephesians 1:18 &19a

God never designed us to walk in darkness. In fact, He made sure that light was available to us before we came into existence.[10] The God of Light is Alpha and Omega. He knows the beginning from the end. He made us to live and reign intelligently and with brilliance, so that no force of darkness could ever overshadow us. If all of this is true, why do we often feel like we are alone and in the dark?

Far too often, things happen that leave us wondering, "Why?" When we can't proffer an answer, the devil jumps at the opportunity to answer it for us. If Satan can get you to accept his answer, he can surely get you to subscribe to his solution. If we are not careful, our ignorance can lead us to death. The Bible says, in Hosea 4:6, that the people of God perish not by sword or demonic attack, but rather "…by lack of knowledge." The devil uses what we don't understand as a foundation to imprint his lies into our minds and to eventually imprint his thought flow into our hearts.

We cannot passively allow Satan to lead us into error by way of ignorance. Revelation gives us the ammunition we need to fight the devil intelligently. God does not desire for any of His children to perish. He has designed life to afford you victory in every situation. By the end of this chapter, you will better understand the purpose and power of revelation knowledge, how to obtain it, and how to use it as a repellent against disruptive imaginations.

THE PURPOSE OF REVELATION

When the trials of life leave you feeling limited, anxious, or cast down, know that it is just that, a feeling. Feelings are fleeting and deceptive. Don't draw conclusions about your situation based on what things feel like, or even what they look like. Instead, ask God for revelation. Revelation is supernatural disclosure from God to us, to prepare us for what's next to help us rightly analyze our current experiences.

Revelation is a repellent to disruptive imaginations and a clarifier, giving us a divine understanding of anything that has to do with our lives and destiny. It's a weapon that guards us against Satan's lies and distortions of reality. When we have revelation knowledge, our minds are occupied with what God has revealed to us. Our risk of entertaining disruptive imaginations reduces dramatically when our minds are not idle. Revelation is a powerful defensive tool, but it is equally an offensive weapon, critical for an effective prayer life and for carrying out your divine assignment as you carry out your walk with God.

REVELATION 101

Revelation knowledge is not optional for a believer in Christ Jesus. It is the vial by which God gives us the truth we need for victorious living. Once you fully accept and confess the truth God has made available to you—genuine revelation of Jesus Christ and His love for you—you can instantly begin to pull down the imaginations tormenting your destiny one by one.

Divine Revelation

You do not need salvation to receive revelation. In fact, it is only by revelation that a person chooses to accept Jesus as both Savior and Lord over their lives. Take your time to study and meditate on John 14, especially verses 1-11. Jesus is the Way, the *Truth*, and the Life. To receive truth and revelation is to receive Him.

> *"...And no one knows who the Father is except the Son and those to whom the Son chooses to reveal him."* Then he turned to his disciples and said privately, *"Blessed are the eyes that see what you see. For I tell you that many prophets and kings wanted to see what you see but did not see it, and to hear what you hear but did not hear it."*
> **Luke 10:22-24**

Accept Christ as your Lord and Savior. Abide in Him and allow His Word to abide in you, and watch as the distraction of the cares of this life evaporates right before your eyes.

QUALIFIERS

Satan wants you to believe that only *special* people qualify to receive revelation knowledge. This is true only if you understand that you and all of God's creation are special to Him. Give God your heart and take on His Holy Spirit. He is eager to reveal to you all of the mysteries of His kingdom.

How do you obtain revelation? Start by reading your Bible and actively seeking the truth. If you are a follower of Christ, nothing should ever come to you as a total surprise. The Bible says, "In all thy getting, get understanding."[11] As you do this, the revelation you need will come and come on time.

God has equipped you with direct access to revelation knowledge. Your habitual practice of spending time in the following avenues guarantees your access to clear, expedited, daily revelation of the truth. You must dwell:

In His Word | In His Presence | In His Service |
In Communication with His Servants

These are all avenues for receiving revelation. Obedience to God's will grants you easy access to revelation. When you spend time in the presence of God as you pray, worship and heed the instruction and information provided to you by God's anointed, you will know how to obey and how to open yourself up to receive revelation from God.

Request It

> *I keep asking that the God of our Lord Jesus Christ, the glorious Father, may give you the Spirit of wisdom and revelation, so that you may know him better.*
>
> **Ephesians 1:17**

"Ask and it shall be given to you..." the Bible tells us in Matthew 7:7. God is our generous Father, who loves to give us good gifts. When you ask any thing in His name and according to His will, rest assured, Jehovah Jireh will give it to you.

Expect It

God is always looking for opportunities to reveal more of Himself to you. Romans 12:12-21 gives us a blueprint of what our attitude should look like, especially when it seems everything is going wrong. The devil will not waste any time before he gives you all the reasons and valid excuses you need to quit. He does not want you to trust God or seek revelation knowledge from His Word.

Don't be moved by your emotions or situations. These things are fleeting. God and His promises remain the same! Set your mind on God and His Word. Remain expectant that God, who promised never to leave or forsake you, is always ready to share His mysteries with you!

Hunger & Thirst After Righteousness

If you are busy fulfilling all righteousness with your whole heart, there is very little time or space for the devil to fill your mind with disruptive imaginations. There is a level of obedience that qualifies you for revelation knowledge. As you hunger and thirst after righteousness as described in Matthew 5:6, God will begin to fill you up with everything you need, including revelation knowledge. When you hunger and thirst for righteousness as the deer pants for water, you demonstrate your willingness to do whatever it takes to live a life that is pleasing to God.

Obedience is one of the greatest qualifiers for everything you need from the Lord. It signifies your love for Him. Your obedience proves to God that He can trust you with information. Your acts of obedience are a sweet-smelling fragrance to Him, and they move Him to count you among the righteous.

Seek Knowledge | Gain Understanding | Obtain Wisdom

> *For the Lord gives wisdom; from his mouth come knowledge and understanding.*
>
> **Proverbs 2:6**

Take time to get your facts straight! Know what the Bible says by reading it in its entirety and in context. Study it. Meditate on it. Confess it. Knowledge does not just come to you. You must earnestly seek it. You must desire it. The more you know what God says about you, the less the devil can tell you.

Seeking out knowledge and understanding eventually affords you wisdom, a major qualifier for obtaining revelation. As you ask God for wisdom, you will find that He begins to reveal to you how and when to apply all that you learn in His

Word. Proverbs 2 further describes the benefits of wisdom, and why God desires that we attain it. Let's look at verses 1-5:

> *My son, if you accept my words and store up my commands within you, turning your ear to wisdom and applying your heart to understanding indeed, if you call out for insight and cry aloud for understanding, and if you look for it as for silver and search for it as for hidden treasure, then you will understand the fear of the Lord and find the knowledge of God.*
>
> **Proverbs 2:1-5**

When you have wisdom, you are more sensitive to what God is doing and what He desires to reveal to you. When you are wise, you fear the Lord, showing Him the kind of honor that qualifies you for revelation. How does one obtain wisdom? The Bible says:

> *The fear of the Lord is the beginning of wisdom, and knowledge of the Holy One is understanding. For through wisdom your days will be many, and years will be added to your life. If you are wise, your wisdom will reward you; if you are a mocker, you alone will suffer.*
>
> **Proverbs 9:10-12**

When the Bible says, "The fear of the Lord is the beginning of wisdom," it is saying that the first thing any truly wise person will do is get to know the Lord, their God. He is the source of everything, so to know Him is to have access to the answers of life's critical questions. Obeying the Word of God and honoring Him in all we do is our first step to obtaining wisdom.

Hope

> *Now faith is confidence in what we hope for and assurance about what we do not see.*
> **Hebrews 11:1**

When we hope, we persevere. We have a basis for faith to increase. If imaginations arise to terrorize us to keep us from moving forward, hope pushes us to advance. When we have hope, we have confidence that something good can still come of the situation. We won't be so easily deceived into accepting a false reality.

> *Why, my soul, are you downcast? Why so disturbed within me? Put your hope in God, for I will yet praise him, my Savior and my God.*
> **Psalm 42:11**

REALITY CHECK

> *Reality (noun): The true situation that exists: the real situation.*
> **© 2019 Merriam-Webster, Inc.**

While reality is visible, what is visible is not always reality. For everything taking place on earth, something has already taken place in the spiritual realm influencing this natural activity. When critical things are happening in our lives, it's easy to believe that the series of events leading to the point of your critical experience is circumstantial. The truth is, Satan is so strategic, he doesn't mind waiting a thousand years for a single result. There are images that he exposed your grandparents to just to influence decisions you will later make in life. You can study Romans 8 or Daniel 10, and many other scriptures, to better understand spiritual dynamics and their role in our earthly lives.

Reality gives relevance to imagination. Let's talk about what we can see vs. reality.

> *Let your eyes look straight ahead; fix your gaze directly before you. Give careful thought to the paths for your feet and be steadfast in all your ways.*
>
> **Proverbs 4:25-26**

What you "set your eyes on" determines how you will advance in life. It is what you can see clearly that lets you know how, when, and where to move. So, before you can do anything, you must have seen something. And if you have seen anything, you can further imagine it. And if you can imagine it, you can make it your reality.

Take a moment to check in with yourself right now. Think about all you have seen recently. How do you feel? What is prompting your current emotional state? Believe it or not, something you have witnessed, consciously or subconsciously, is influencing the current state of your mind. The question is, what exactly did you allow yourself to see?

> *I lift up my eyes to the mountains—where does my help come from? My help comes from the Lord, the Maker of heaven and earth.*
>
> **Psalm 121:1-2**

Set your eyes on God. He is Alpha and Omega. He is your Creator and Helper. Because of the gift of His Son,

Jesus Christ, you have hope. The things you allow yourself to see are the things you'll think about. It's what you think about regularly that will form your reality. "For as he thinks in his heart, so is he" (Proverbs 23:7 NKJV).

> *So we don't look at the troubles we can see now; rather, we fix our gaze on things that cannot be seen. For the things we see now will soon be gone, but the things we cannot see will last forever.*
>
> ### 2 Corinthians 4:18 (NLT)

It is as we *"set our eyes"* on trouble that evil imaginations have license to take shape and take over. When we allow things to ruminate in our minds and hearts, we allow them to shape our spirits. The spirit we carry determines how we interpret situations and how we will operate with the information we receive.

REVELATIONS YOU MUST HAVE:

Ephesians 6:10-20 gives us our game plan for withstanding Satan's schemes. The first piece of equipment God tells us to put on is the "Belt of Truth." It keeps you free from the physical, spiritual, and psychological damage caused by lies and deception. You have access to the revelation knowledge of the gospel truth. Use it to your advantage!

Revelation knowledge ensures that you are neither surprised nor confused about what's happening concerning you, your family, or the body of Christ. The devil's tactics aren't brand new. Reading your Bible alone opens you up to the truth. As you study the Word of God, you gain knowledge.

As you meditate on it, you receive understanding and wisdom. Once you develop your understanding and you learn to apply it, you demonstrate your hunger for wisdom and righteousness. This opens you up to receive revelation.

You will first receive revelation concerning all that you have studied and meditated upon. Then, over time, or maybe at once, you begin to receive deeper, more specific revelations. These revelations include clarity concerning things that have happened in the past. A revelation of past events is critical for two reasons. The first is so that mistakes aren't repeated, or so that you know what to do or how to receive it when it occurs again. The second critical reason is so that you are conscious of the resultant effects of what has taken place, and you are prepared to respond accordingly.

You will receive revelation about what is happening at present. Before the devil can interpret things for you, you will already have an understanding, so that you do not do or say things that disrupt what God wants to bring out of that situation for your good.

Finally, you will receive revelation of events ahead. Your future is bright! God knows it. The devil knows it. But most importantly, you must know it so that you will always have hope and stay well-prepared and ready to fight with the outlook that you have already received the victory. When you know what is ahead, you will give more time to praise and worship and less time to worry. Having revelation knowledge concerning your future shields you from anxiety, stress, worry, and those things that keep many people in our generation down today.

God has given you the truth about matters. You only need to believe it and receive it! I implore you to study your Bible to know what God has already said concerning you. Don't just read it once. Read it again and again, and then meditate on it. Once you believe it, confess it. Let the devil hear your awareness! For optimal results, please take your time to read and confess daily. Focus especially on confessing His Word as related to problems you have encountered in life, and problems that have bothered your family or your forefathers over the years. This keeps you safe and wards off the devil.

I said this before, and I must say it again: The devil isn't really doing anything new. He is just presenting his old tricks to you in new ways so you will likely receive them. The next few pages contain common disruptive imaginations, and the countering revelation knowledge that you must have concerning them according to scripture. Study the Word, and I am certain you will come up with many more! As you continue to develop a habit of reading, meditating, and confessing God's Word, may you be opened up to an overflow of divine revelation knowledge in Jesus Christ's name!

CASTING DOWN

IMAGINED LONELINESS

- Never will I leave you; never will I forsake you. **Hebrews 13:5b (NIV)**
- And the Lord, He is the One who goes before you. He will be with you, He will not leave you nor forsake you; do not fear nor be dismayed. **-Deuteronomy 31:8 (NKJV)**

IMAGINED HELPLESSNESS/ VICTIMIZATION

- No, in all these things we are more than conquerors through him who loved us. **Romans 8:37 (NIV)**
- Blessed be the Lord my strength which teacheth my hands to war, and my fingers to fight: My goodness, and my fortress; my high tower, and my deliverer; my shield, and he in whom I trust; who subdueth my people under me. **Psalm 144:1-2 (KJV)**

IMAGINED USELESSNESS

- For we are His workmanship, created in Christ Jesus for good works, which God prepared beforehand that we should walk in them. **Ephesians 2:10 (NKJV)**
- Your eyes saw my substance, being yet unformed. And in Your book they all were written, the days fashioned for me, when as yet there were none of them. How precious also are Your thoughts to me, O God! How great is the sum of them! **Psalm 139:16-17 (NKJV)**
- Are not two sparrows sold for a copper coin? And not one of them falls to the ground apart from your Father's will. But the very hairs of your head are all numbered. Do not fear therefore; you are of more value than many sparrows. **Matthew 10:29-31 (NKJV)**

IMAGINED HOPELESSNESS

- For I know the thoughts that I think toward you, says the Lord, thoughts of peace and not of evil, to give you a future and a hope. **Jeremiah 29:11 (NKJV)**

IMAGINED REJECTION

- Though my father and mother forsake me, the Lord will receive me. **Psalm 27:10 (NIV)**

IMAGINED POVERTY

- And God is able to bless you abundantly, so that in all things at all times, having all that you need, you will abound in every good work. **2 Corinthians 9:8 (NIV)**
- And my God will meet all your needs according to the riches of his glory in Christ Jesus. **Phillipians 4:19 (NIV)**

▶ IMAGINED FAILURE

- But he said to me, "My grace is sufficient for you, for my power is made perfect in weakness." Therefore I will boast all the more gladly about my weaknesses, so that Christ's power may rest on me. That is why, for Christ's sake, I delight in weaknesses, in insults, in hardships, in persecutions, in difficulties. For when I am weak, then I am strong. - **2 Corinthians 12:9 (NIV)**
- I can do all things through him who strengthens me. - **Phillipians 4:13 (ESV)**

▶ IMAGINED STRESSORS

- Count it all joy, my brothers, when you meet trials of various kinds, for you know that the testing of your faith produces steadfastness. And let steadfastness have its full effect, that you may be perfect and complete, lacking in nothing. **James 1:2-4 (ESV)**
- Peace I leave with you; my peace I give you. I do not give to you as the world gives. Do not let your hearts be troubled and do not be afraid. **John 14:27 (NIV)**
- "Come to me, all you who are weary and burdened, and I will give you rest. Take my yoke upon you and learn from me, for I am gentle and humble in heart, and you will find rest for your souls. For my yoke is easy and my burden is light." **Matthew 11:28-30 (NIV)**

▶ IMAGINED BARENNESS

- Shout for joy, O barren one, you who have borne no child; Break forth into joyful shouting and cry aloud, you who have not travailed; For the sons of the desolate one will be more numerous than the sons of the married woman," says the LORD. **Isaiah 54:1 (NASB)**

▶ IMAGINED SUFFERING

- I consider that our present sufferings are not worth comparing with the glory that will be revealed in us. **Romans 8:18 (NIV)**

▶ IMAGINED CONFLICT

- We are hard pressed on every side, but not crushed; perplexed, but not in despair; persecuted, but not abandoned; struck down, but not destroyed. We always carry around in our body the death of Jesus, so that the life of Jesus may also be revealed in our body. **2 Corinthians 4:8-10 (NIV)**

▶ IMAGINED GUILT

- Therefore, there is now no condemnation for those who are in Christ Jesus, because through Christ Jesus the law of the Spirit who gives life has set you free from the law of sin and death. **Romans 8:1-2 (NIV)**

▶ IMAGINED SICKNESS/DEATH

- For God so loved that world that He gave his only begotten Son, that whoever believes in Him should not perish but have everlasting life. **John 3:16 (NKJV)**
- For we who are alive are always being given over to death for Jesus' sake, so that his life may also be revealed in our mortal body. So then, death is at work in us, but life is at work in you. **2 Corinthians 4:11-12 (NIV)**

CHAPTER FIVE

THE HIGH AND EXALTED THINGS

He removed the high places, smashed the sacred stones and cut down the Asherah poles. He broke into pieces the bronze snake Moses had made, for up to that time the Israelites had been burning incense to it.

2 Kings 18:4

O nce upon a time, when I was just a little girl in a very lonely place, I made an acquaintance: *self-pity*. It didn't take long for self-pity and me to form a strong bond that I thought would last forever. Before I knew it, she was there every time my feelings were hurt. She was there to mourn with me every time I gazed at other families, only to see that any chance I had at a "normal" life with a "normal" family had died with the sudden dissolution of my parents' marriage.

Self-pity was there when it seemed no one else was, and she dutifully followed me from my home in Michigan all the way to my new, unexpectedly motherless life in Nigeria.

It's hard to believe that this dark acquaintance I had made so early in life would become my best friend! Self-pity was dependable and was always there. I loved her!

Self-pity and I lived together and were inseparable. She was always with me, and I became fully dependent on her. She gave me the biggest pity parties imaginable. Her voice was strong throughout my teenage years and into early adulthood. She was even at my wedding. She continued to be there for me, rendering advice and helping me see things as only she could for the first few years of my marriage. Our relationship became the lens by which I learned to interpret everything I experienced. We were so close that I couldn't see how much she'd cost me over the years. If not for divine revelation, she could have cost me everything.

* * *

When we talk about the "high and exalted things," we are talking about everything that we foolishly give glory to, consciously or unconsciously. It is what you give glory to that becomes lord over your life. Nothing should be greater than God in our lives.

The explanation I gave you about my dealings with self-pity may sound dramatic, but this is exactly what it looks like when imaginations become high and exalted things. Once exalted, you grant them permission to form strongholds over you.

EXALTATION

Exaltation is a very specific type of praise that carries two agendas, the most obvious being a genuine expression of honor and gratitude for one's generous contribution to our lives. Christians have many songs and psalms to help us carry out our innate desire to *exalt* the name of the Lord, our God. Why shouldn't we? Indeed, He is worthy to be praised! Jesus explains the second function of exaltation in the book of John when He proclaims:

> *And I, if I be lifted from the earth, will draw all men unto me.*
> **John 12:32 (KJV)**

When we exalt the name of the Lord, we are doing more than acknowledging that He is rightfully seated in majesty at the right hand of the Father. We are carrying out the divine mandate given to us when we give our lives to Him.[12]

THEY ALL FALL DOWN

> *For those who exalt themselves will be humbled, and those who humble themselves will be exalted.*
> **Matthew 23:12**

God created everything for a predetermined time and purpose. He then placed it, strategically, wherever He needed it to be to fulfill His plans. Lucifer trailblazed the habit of abuse. Abuse means that something is being used for reasons it was not created for, ultimately leading to disruption, dysfunction, and/or destruction.

> *How art thou fallen from heaven, O, Lucifer, son of the morning! How art thou cut down to the ground, which didst weaken the nations!*

For thou hast said in thine heart, I will ascend into heaven, I will exalt my throne above the stars of God: I will sit also upon the mount of the congregation, in the sides of the north: I will ascend above the heights of the clouds; I will be like the most High.

Isaiah 14:12-14 (KJV)

When he decided that he could be what he was never created to be, the way was paved for all of creation to opt for the same opportunity. God allowed it to be so, for our sakes.

We human beings were designed like our Creator. Although Satan, in envy and rage, tries to deter us at every turn, he is also our alternative, proving that we could choose just how God-like we desired to be—if we chose to be like Him at all. How privileged we are! Lucifer was not so privileged. As we will learn, everything that finds itself out of place must be removed.

If the item or entity has been placed illegally on high, its removal involves a terrible fall.

Yet thou shalt be brought down to hell, to the sides of the pit. They that see thee shall narrowly look upon thee, and consider thee, saying, Is this the man that made the earth to tremble, that did shake kingdoms; That made the world as a wilderness, and destroyed the cities thereof; that opened not the house of his prisoners?

Isaiah 14:15-17 (KJV)

Satan is your defeated foe. The moment you see him and his schemes as such, casting down disruptive imaginations and pulling down strongholds will not seem like an impossible task to you.

> *He replied, "I saw Satan fall like lightning from heaven. I have given you authority to trample on snakes and scorpions and to overcome all the power of the enemy; nothing will harm you. However, do not rejoice that the spirits submit to you, but rejoice that your names are written in heaven."*
>
> **Luke 10:18-20**

You have the authority, ability, and responsibility to bring down every high and exalted thing in your path.

CASE STUDY I

> *…He did what was right in the eyes of the Lord, just as his father David had done. He removed the high places, smashed the sacred stones and cut down the Asherah poles. He broke into pieces the bronze snake Moses had made, for up to that time the Israelites had been burning incense to it. (It was called Nehushtan). Hezekiah trusted in the Lord, the God of Israel. There was no one like him among all the kings of Judah, either before him or after him. He held fast to the Lord and did not stop following him; He kept the commands the Lord had given Moses. And the Lord was with him; he was successful in whatever he undertook. He rebelled against the king of Assyria and did not serve him. From watchtower to fortified city, he*

defeated the Philistines, as far as Gaza and its territory.

2 Kings 18:3-8

Hezekiah had every reason not to make the choices he did. Because he was exposed to the truth, he understood that it was his responsibility to put things back in order. This is the mentality we must have. Idolatry is cancerous. There is a reason why God did not want the Israelites to live amongst people who practiced it. Likewise, it's a dangerous thing for you to surround yourself with people who exalt anything or any being above the Lord. No matter how holy you are, spending too much time in the wrong environment without the spiritual strength to change that environment can land you in a state you should not find yourself in.

IDOLATRY

We cannot sit idly by and accept idolatry in our lives because it's the cultural norm, or "the times we live in." As Hezekiah demonstrated, you equally have the God-given authority and responsibility to change things, both in your life and in your environment. Today's society emphasizes "coping." Practice "feeling better" about the state of today's affairs, even though it's harming you. Buy $300 headphones, play with slime and stress balls, idolize your smart phone or your car or social media. Do whatever makes you feel better about the darkness claiming territory in your life.

You just found a new show that has four whole seasons, thirteen episodes each. A little binge watching is not a sin. Life is so overwhelming. You need to decompress from all its stress. You'll only watch four episodes today. But four episodes became fourteen before you recognized it. Then, you had to find another series to explore. Then, you sacrificed a few nights of sleep and altered your schedule to accommodate your "decompression" time. Soon, seeing "what happens next" became your priority. Finally, you have finished three whole series when you remember that it's been awhile since you were quite productive or had your quiet time with the Lord.

You must be at work at 5:30 a.m. You spent hours shopping and can't afford to spend time with the God of your salvation or work towards your goals in life; you are not too far from practicing idolatry. You're exalting your senses above your Savior. What are you obsessed with? Be careful! Your obsession can easily become a high and exalted thing in your life, and this is how idolatry begins. If you don't correct it, like every misplaced high thing, it ends in downfall.

CASE STUDY II

When you find yourself in a predicament that is peculiar, there are at least two reports you can subscribe to: What God says, and what the situation says.

There is the case of Abraham and Sarah. They received a promise from God that Abraham would become the father of many nations. They had what God said. Yet, their situation said that both Abraham and Sarah were beyond an age when bearing children was possible.

We know from scripture that although they both had faith for the promise, they tried to help God along by using Sarah's handmaid, Hagar, to birth the promise. As a result, they bore Ishmael, which, to date, bears evidence of the impact of man getting things done by his own effort.[13] It took more than twenty-five years for God's promise to manifest, but Isaac was born, and eventually Jacob...and the twelve tribes of Israel, which included the lineage through which our Lord and Savior would be birthed.[14]

THE EXALTATION OF IMAGINATIONS

What God says might not be visible or seem logical, but what is visible might not be the full picture and does not consider the "unseen things" or the things that are to come. You will likely choose based on your experiences and exposure. Whichever report you choose is indicative of your exposure and experiences over time.

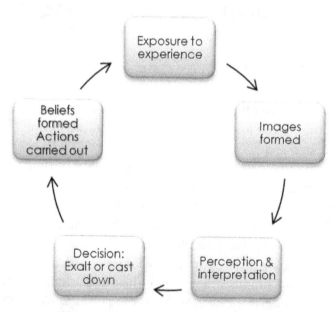

Figure 2 The cycle of images formed and imaginations rising to be exalted or cast down.

Although what is imagined has never seen reality, something very real happened to provoke it, leaving images behind for the mind to interpret. Images are an embodiment or imprint of what is real. For those who do not know something, an image gives them a visual to help them relate to it.

Images are designed to evoke emotion, understanding, and action, based on the knowledge of who or what it represents. Images provide their audience with insight and information. Without images, it would be quite difficult for us to relate to or understand many things. Imagination is not all bad. As a matter of fact, when it is propelled by the right force, imagination is necessary for advancement. But here is where imaginations become a problem:

> The LORD observed the extent of human wickedness on the earth, and he saw that everything they thought or imagined was consistently and totally evil.
>
> **Genesis 6:5 (NLT)**

Wherever Satan is allowed, there will be evil. He cannot create anything. What he can do is influence your perception and understanding of things, if you allow him the opportunity. As unreal as imaginations are, your reality depends on your engagement of them. Any thoughts you entertain more than your thoughts pertaining to the kingdom of God and His plan for your life *must* be cast down! If they are not cast down, they will grow into imaginations. The imaginations formed will compel you to exalt them until they eventually become strongholds.

NO MORE DISRUPTION

SEGMENT TWO

PREVIEW II

WINGS LIKE AN EAGLE

They will soar on wings like eagles; they will run and not grow weary; they will walk and not be faint.

Isaiah 40:31

As a member of God's family, you have a divine advantage. This advantage is an ability that is embedded in your DNA as a believer. It remains engrained in you until the moment you find yourself in the fullness of God's presence for eternity and have no need of anything else. God created you to ***soar***!

Once your covenant relationship with God, our Father, is ignited, your spirit man is equipped to elevate you high above the impact and influence of natural affairs. Immediately, as you imbibe your portion of Christ's unyielding salvation, you become as an eagle, graced to see sharply and soar fiercely above the world's winds, towards your mark. The Holy Spirit is your advantage! He is your ability. As He abides in you, your spirit is empowered to soar and to lead you from glory to glory, guiding every one of your steps in the right direction!

We have established, now, that the Spirit of God ushers your spirit man into a state of leadership over your earthly life, making it possible for you to soar in every circumstance.

> *In a desert land he found him, in a barren and howling waste. He shielded him and cared for him; he guarded him as the apple of his eye, like an eagle that stirs up its nest and hovers over its young, that spreads its wings to catch them and carries them aloft. The Lord alone led him; no foreign god was with him.*
>
> **Deuteronomy 32:10-12**

CHAPTER SIX

HOW TO ENGAGE THE
WEAPONS OF OUR WARFARE

For the weapons of our warfare are not carnal,
but mighty through God to the pulling down of
strong holds.

2 Corinthians 10:4 (KJV)

It is in our nature to look for physical solutions to supernatural problems. Satan enjoys it when we fail to recognize that the challenges we are experiencing are not of
this world. He would much rather you waste time, energy,
and resources spending money to figure out why you always
get a migraine when it's time for you to study, or consider
separation, divorce, or misery because your spouse doesn't
seem to honor you.

I stated this earlier on and will state it again: God loves
you and does not desire for you or any of His children to suffer. When things are going awry, remember that everything
happening naturally has a supernatural trigger. You must find
out what it is.

IDENTIFY THE TRIGGERS

There are some general moments in time known to trigger disruptive imaginations. The devil strategically assigns certain demonic activity to take place at very routine times. Most times, it happens when we should be expressing gratitude or celebrating successes. I had a friend who would get beautiful flowers on her birthday. I would see them and think, *Wow, her husband must really love her!*

Before I knew it, my thoughts of admiration mutated into a distorted interpretation of the experience I was having in my own life. I went from seeing the beautiful bouquet of flowers my friend received to thinking, *He must love her far more than my husband loves me. Why doesn't my husband buy me flowers? Doesn't he think I'm special?* Instantly, I would begin to feel sorry for myself. Negative thoughts would flood my mind and completely distort my perception of the true relationship I had with my husband. As a matter of fact, I preferred the gifts he gave me, because fresh-cut flowers eventually die, and his expensive gifts lasted for years! The truth is, I would have been upset if he had bought me big bouquets of flowers instead of the gifts he got me! Triggers toy with our emotions and present us with things we may not really want or need. The goal of triggers is to distort and negatively impact our ability to think clearly and biblically.

Once God helped me see the pattern, I found my triggers. I would always feel sorry for myself when I saw married couples expressing their care for one another differently than I experienced with my husband. I traced it back to my childhood and the trauma of experiencing my parents' divorce, and all the disruption that brought into my life. Identifying this trigger helped me to think about why I felt the way that I did. It helped me to pinpoint my vulnerabilities—the places where healing and resolve was needed.

Identifying triggers forced me to reconcile all the feelings of rejection and feeling "less than" that I had embraced as a child. Once I recognized it, I equipped myself accordingly with God's word of truth. When the enemy tried to bring such disruption my way again, I wasted no time casting that thought from my mind, and I continued to do so until the devil grew weary and conceded. I overcame that battle!

As human beings, it's part of our adamic nature to fall back into the sinful state we were born into, no matter how long we have been born again. If we experience fear to the point of developing a spirit of fear, we can cast it out, sure, but it will always return—*except* when we have filled the vacant space with faith.

THE WAR WITHIN

Satan is your adversary. He is not happy that you are made in God's likeness and image. He is not happy that one made from the dirt of the earth was designed to carry such dominion. Satan aspired to be like God and to even reign above Him. When his plans failed, he resolved that by any means, you must fail too. Once you get this revelation—that the devil is warring against you—you will not see your decisions in life as personal and common, but as part of a war strategy, and you will make better choices, including not wasting your time entertaining or allowing disruptive imaginations to torment your life. You will understand that you must fight!

The Battleground

Your mind is a battleground. It's the place where the devil, in all his cunning ways, chooses to fight you, because it is where you are weakest. He understands that with God, you already have the victory. He wants to get you to believe that either you are undeserving of a relationship with God, or that you don't need it—whatever will keep you from Him, so that you are without the truth and without defense. This is why the Holy Scripture encourages us to renew our minds, which we will talk more about in subsequent chapters.

Victory Through Christ Jesus

Your relationship with Christ comes with benefits, such as discernment, compassion, grace, and so much more! The greatest benefit you obtain from this relationship is victory! Your win is assured when Christ is your ally.

The battle for your life began thousands of years ago. Before you were conceived, Christ went to war for you. He took the keys from hell, ensuring that you could overcome the laws of sin and death. With Jesus, you cannot be overtaken or held captive by anything.

What do you have victory over? Besides death, hell, and the grave, you have victory over everything the enemy throws your way! You have victory over every thought and imagination that is not from God. You have victory over the spirit of fear!

> *"Be strong and courageous. Do not be afraid or terrified because of them, for the Lord your God goes with you; he will never leave you nor for-*

sake you." Then Moses summoned Joshua and said to him in the presence of all Israel, "Be strong and courageous, for you must go with this people into the land that the Lord swore to their ancestors to give them, and you must divide it among them as their inheritance.

The Lord himself goes before you and will be with you; he will never leave you nor forsake you. Do not be afraid; do not be discouraged."

Deuteronomy 31:6-8

God has equipped you with every resource you need to win in life; you only need to take hold of your weapons and fight! This is easier said than done, because of the condition of our minds. You must remain conscious of the use of your brain as the devil's preferred workspace. You cannot leave your mind vulnerable to his attacks. Study the scriptures below.

For those who live according to the flesh set their minds on the things of the flesh, but those who live according to the Spirit set their minds on the things of the Spirit.

Romans 8:5 (ESV)

Finally, brothers, whatever is true, whatever is honorable, whatever is just, whatever is pure, whatever is lovely, whatever is commendable, if there is any excellence, if there is anything worthy of praise, think about these things.

Philippians 4:8 (ESV)

These scriptures implore us to keep our minds occupied on the things of God. With Him and what He has spoken concerning us on our minds, there is little room for the devil to cloud our judgment with disruptive imaginations. As you set the atmosphere of your mind to victory in Christ Jesus, it becomes easier to recognize, instantly, when thoughts are not of God, prompting you to cast them out at once.

YOUR WEAPONS

For the weapons of our warfare are not carnal, but mighty through God to the pulling down of strong holds.
2 Corinthians 10:4 (KJV)

So, what are these weapons? The devil doesn't mind when we solve our problems naturally, because anything that is natural has an expiration date. He wants you to spend your resources on things that aren't necessarily bad, but costly over time, with limited results. Medicine, therapy, and indulging in comforting activities can all make you feel better, but your relief will not necessarily be permanent—and more importantly, none of these things are foolproof against demonic attack.

Friends, please make sure you develop a strong understanding of 2 Corinthians 10:4. It is paramount for victorious living. God does not want us to waste time or resources trying to solve spiritual problems with natural solutions. Doing so will only leave you frustrated and in a condition far worse than before.

Finally, be strong in the Lord and in his mighty power. Put on the full armor of God, so that you

can take your stand against the devil's schemes.
For our struggle is not against flesh and blood,
but against the rulers, against the authori-
ties, against the powers of this dark world and
against the spiritual forces of evil in the heav-
enly realms. Therefore put on the full armor of
God, so that when the day of evil comes, you
may be able to stand your ground, and after you
have done everything, to stand.

Ephesians 6:10-13

Ephesians 6:10-17 defines our weapons and their purpose for us. With any weapon, natural or physical, you must train and practice for accuracy. Let's look at our weapons to know how, when, and why to use them in general.

YOUR AMMUNITION

Spiritual weapons do not operate like natural weapons that run out with every use. The more you use your spiritual weapons, they, like everything in the kingdom of God, produce an increase. As you develop the habit of remaining fully equipped with the armor God has made available to you, you will notice an increase in your ammunition—that is, the fruits of the Spirit. Your ammunition has the power to change the whole atmosphere, bringing everything unto the subjection of the Holy Spirit.

The higher your level of ammunition, the lower the probability of you ever being overpowered by disruptive spirits, imaginations, or strongholds.

Figure 3 Ammunition: Our Fruits of the Holy Spirit

DIVINE STRATEGY

> *If then you have been raised with Christ, seek*
> *the things that are above, where Christ is, seated*
> *at the right hand of God. Set your minds on*
> *things that are above, not on things that are on*
> *earth.*

Colossians 3:1-2 (ESV)

Remember, a stronghold is a mighty configuration designed to withstand the toughest blows. Once erected, a spiritual stronghold poses an ongoing threat to any territory where it has been established. They are easier to prevent than eradicate. You can have all the biblical and spiritual knowledge in the world, but you will not be able to withstand the impact of a stronghold in isolation and without a divinely executed strategy.

We establish the method by which we can get rid of both strongholds and disruptive imaginations with this scripture:

> *The weapons we fight with are not the weapons*
> *of the world. On the contrary, they have divine*
> *power to demolish strongholds.*
> **2 Corinthians 10:4**

Every spiritual thing that impacts the earth requires divine partnership. Because God gave us dominion on earth, spiritual activity, in general, can only happen with human permission. Our weapons and strategies aren't carnal, because the altercation is not with us. As much as everything impacts us, it's not about us, specifically. God has given us His divine nature and spiritual weapons so that we can partake in the victory over Satan and his dark kingdom. God has already gone ahead of us. Our overcoming and triumph are sure!

Just as with any prophecy, knowing the outcome does not absolve us of partaking in the process. Our execution of divine strategy is critical not only for the assurance of victory, but also for the assurance of our godly character. Your compliance to this method of training builds your credibility with God, strengthens you for overcoming future temptations, and prepares you to fulfill your God-given assignment on earth.

Our strategy against the kingdom of darkness requires us to partner with the Holy Spirit to implement both offensive and defensive strategies of combat.

Offensive Strategy

> *For the Spirit God gave us does not make us timid, but gives us power, love and self-discipline.*
> **2 Timothy 1:7**

You were designed as a force of influence. When God created you, He equipped you with the capacity to make things happen. As surely as God makes all things new, you, as one made in His image, can make a difference wherever you find yourself. Adaptability is very important and necessary at times. But did you know that you never really have to adapt to places or situations? The truth is that they must adapt to you! The Spirit of God in you is always greater than any other spirit in any other place. You can change environments and circumstances.

> *But you will receive power when the Holy Spirit comes on you; and you will be my witnesses in Jerusalem, and in all Judea and Samaria, and to the ends of the earth.*
> **Acts 1:8**

The Holy Spirit empowers you to influence situations. It is important that you increase and consistently engage in spiritual activities, so that the Holy Spirit continues to increase in you. Spiritual activities include studying your Bible and praying, especially in the Spirit.

Blood has power. It connects you to a legacy and an inheritance. It binds, gives life, heals, and separates. Both the name of Jesus and the blood of Jesus are purposed to be used proactively and as needed against strongholds and disruptive imaginations. Every weapon discussed earlier must be used with your God-given authority. This authority is backed up with the name of Jesus Christ. Christ's perfect execution of the work of redemption affords us power from both His blood and His name. Think about a person who is the blood relative of the president of the United States or any country. Those known to be blood relatives stand to gain much and lose much, based on that president's reputation.

> *Listen carefully: I have given you authority [that you now possess] to tread on serpents and scorpions, and [the ability to exercise authority] over all the power of the enemy (Satan); and nothing will [in any way] harm you.*
> **Luke 10:19 (AMP)**

The Word of God is also an instrument of power and authority that you carry. Christ Himself is the Word of God. His life not only gave us everlasting life, but it gives us the authority to speak life into situations as needed. It is the answer and final say concerning the human experience. What the Bible says is always the authority when the prognosis must be determined.

YOUR TONGUE

The application of the blood of Jesus, the name of Jesus, and the Word of God is by word of mouth. Your tongue is a weapon of mass destruction and the determiner of your final experience.

> *Therefore God exalted him to the highest place and gave him the name that is above every name, that at the name of Jesus every knee should bow, in heaven and on earth and under the earth, and every tongue acknowledge that Jesus Christ is Lord, to the glory of God the Father.*
>
> **Philippians 2:9-11**

> *From the fruit of their mouth a person's stomach is filled; with the harvest of their lips they are satisfied. The tongue has the power of life and death, and those who love it will eat its fruit.*
>
> **Proverbs 18:20-21**

Defensive Strategy

Offensive strategies are powerful, and it is a wonder to see the outcomes of those who employ such strategies in the kingdom of God. But even better are the strategies that keep us from falling prey to demonic attack. The defensive strategies God has designed for us produce a myriad of benefits for all who employ them—the most important being a strengthened spiritual life. Remember, kingdom activities, when done habitually and with a sincere heart, take you from strength to strength and from glory to glory. These strategies verify your spiritual growth and aid you in defending your victory over the powers of darkness. Remember, the battle is already won! You don't have to fight to obtain the victory; but be prepared, spiritually, as you will need to fight in order to defend it. Let's look at three critical defensive strategies we must use and use often:

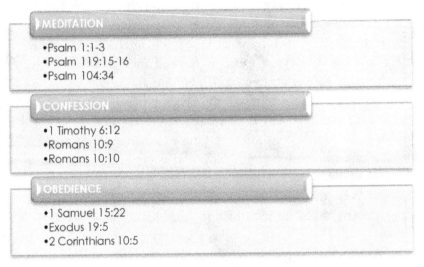

MEDITATION
- Psalm 1:1-3
- Psalm 119:15-16
- Psalm 104:34

CONFESSION
- 1 Timothy 6:12
- Romans 10:9
- Romans 10:10

OBEDIENCE
- 1 Samuel 15:22
- Exodus 19:5
- 2 Corinthians 10:5

Figure 4

MEDITATION

> *Finally, brothers and sisters, whatever is true,*
> *whatever is noble, whatever is right, whatever*
> *is pure, whatever is lovely, whatever is admira-*
> *ble—if anything is excellent or praiseworthy—*
> *think about such things.*
> **Philippians 4:8**

God promises us in His Word that if we "take every thought captive" and give Him all our fears, hurts, disappointments, anxieties, confusion, insecurities, etc., He will remove them "as far as the east is from the west," and He will "meet all our needs."

Take control of your mind before the devil does. What you think becomes what you believe, and what you believe becomes your reality. To meditate is to allow your mind to intentionally focus on one thing for a period. To have the mind of Christ requires you to meditate on His Word. Make this a habit. If your mind is focused on Christ and His thoughts concerning you and your situation, you leave no room for the devil to take over. The key to using meditation as a defensive strategy is your daily habit. As you devote time to study God's Word, devote time to meditate on what He has said concerning you—daily, and as often during the day as possible.

May the Lord strengthen and empower you from His glorious, unlimited resources, in Jesus' name.

CONFESSION

You have whatever you say that you have. The Bible says that God's Word is sharper than any two-edged sword.[3] Therefore, what God says is what you ought to say to guarantee victory over the devil. Your daily confession is a major defensive weapon. What you say now dictates your outcome in the days ahead. If you have children, start declaring God's grace over their lives now. Start speaking concerning their jobs, education, future spouses, even your grandchildren. Start teaching them how to speak God's Word over their lives now. If your confession is negative, you are opening a door for Satan to use your words to wreak havoc in your life. Your tongue is both a defensive and offensive weapon of mass destruction. Use it wisely.

---

[3] Hebrews 4:12

OBEDIENCE

We demolish arguments and every pretension that sets itself up against the knowledge of God, and we take captive every thought to make it obedient to Christ.
2 Corinthians 10:5

Obedience to God's Word is a major strategy against demonic attack and the causes of depression. This strategy is a clever one, because words, like obedience, are not popular. It's a word looked at by others as weak. The truth is, your level of obedience to God and His Word is both an indicator and an increaser of your level of spiritual development. Let's talk more about why obedience is such a grand strategy of God for this world.

Prelude

The eyes of the LORD search the whole earth in order to strengthen those whose hearts are fully committed to him. What a fool you have been!
2 Chronicles 16:9 (NLT)

Most Christians believe that the devil is our greatest enemy. He is our enemy indeed, but one of the greatest battles you will fight in your life is the battle against your own flesh. Your human nature is rebellious by default. We are born into a world of sin, and automatically we take on the ways of the world until we are taught differently.

Satan's goal is to keep Christians in a constant state of mental instability. One state he would like us to stay in is a state of double-mindedness. To be double-minded is to lead two kinds of lives. Your lifestyle and stance on matters changes with your situation or environment.

The devil also loves to keep you in ignorance. He doesn't mind you being religious. He does not even mind if you identify as a Christian. What he does not want is for you to become conscious of your authority that is in Christ Jesus. He will go to any lengths he can to get us to give ourselves over to our own thoughts and emotions, rather than taking those thoughts captive and dealing with them.

To be double-minded means we are living two lives. God's life is in our heart, but it has become quenched and blocked because of our emotional choices. Therefore, self-life is being shown forth in our soul.

The Power of Obedience

> *He has shown you, O mortal, what is good. And what does the LORD require of you? To act justly and to love mercy and to walk humbly with your God.*
>
> **Micah 6:8**

More than He desires sacrifice from us, the Lord desires our obedience. Why? As you just read, we are prone to sin and rebellion. Our habitual obedience to God's Word not only keeps us safe, it builds our Christian character, strengthens our spirit man, and builds our trust with God. As we walk in obedience to God, we become focused on pleasing Him. We have no time for the cares of this life, and it is much more difficult for the devil to lead us astray. Our minds are not idle. Our thoughts are anchored in service to God as we serve Him, grateful for all He has done for us.

Think about an effective army. It consists of a general, a colonel, lieutenants, and subsequent layers of leadership. There are trained soldiers, and there is a strategy. In the army of the Lord, God is the general, working in perfect harmony with the Holy Spirit and Christ, His Son. The captains and lieutenants are the men of God who have been ordained to pastor and guide us in life. In a family setting, Ephesians 6 explains to us that the parents are the captains over their children, whom they must train, equip, and instruct.

Now, the first thing the general does is establish a foundation of trust and expectations through rigorous training with his commanders. The commanders are then charged with rearing up capable soldiers. What makes a soldier worthy of honor is not his intelligence or strength. It's his accuracy in obedience. A soldier's capacity to be completely obedient could mean the difference between life or death.

Likewise, as a believer, you are expected to be like a good soldier. You must yield to godly authority and accept godly correction without taking offense. This keeps you safe. When you are obedient, just like a soldier, God can give you instructions and commands that will guide you around and away from Satan's snares.

CHAPTER SEVEN

HOW TO SIDESTEP A SET-UP

My sheep listen to my voice; I know them, and they follow me. I give them eternal life, and they shall never perish; no one will snatch them out of my hand. My Father, who has given them to me, is greater than all; no one can snatch them out of my Father's hand. I and the Father are one."

John 10:27-30

"Why are you like this?" my close friends would ask me. I could not give an answer at all. All I knew is that I had been "like this" for a very long time. I was not happy, and I felt helpless to change the course of events in my life.

I knew in my heart that if I kept going this way, there would be destruction. But what if we were destined for failure anyway? Was not my parents' marriage destined for failure? Was divorce not the outcome of more than half of the marriages in the United States? Perhaps the dissolution of our union was inevitable.

Meanwhile, I had all these thoughts and feelings bottled up in my heart. "Why am I like this?" I also often asked myself. At the time, I experienced this line of questioning as condescending. In fact, it fed my self-pity. But now, I know better, and I understand that this was the best self-reflective question I could have ever asked myself. It is this same question I proffer to you and to everyone who finds themselves in a place of gloom and hopelessness. Ask yourself, "Why am I like this?" and get to the root of what's driving you.

Friends, every problem, thought, and belief has a root, and it is imperative that you identify it. When you can't identify the root, you are destined to suffer outcomes beyond your control, and that is not the life God designed for His children on the earth. We are designed to be victors. We are designed with power, authority, and dominion by a God who equips us with everything we need for a godly life.

THE SETUP

Satan is very subtle. We are often oblivious to the snares he sets right before our very eyes. When I found myself in situations as described at the commencement of this chapter, I was blind to the fact that the trap I was falling into was handcrafted by Satan more than twenty years prior. I did not recognize that this was a trap that I willingly had subscribed to all those years before. It's like blindly signing a contract because you have a dire need, only to realize that the price you will pay comes with an unfathomable interest rate you will never be able to pay back, leaving you in a predicament far worse than your original dilemma. This is what happened to me, and it is what happens to many of us.

Twenty years ago, I subscribed to this little voice inside that could foretell disaster from a mile away. At the time, that voice felt like protection. When one has become acquainted with fear and anxiety, the devil's promotional ad for such a voice seems like a deal. Something will tell me when to avoid a situation or raise a complaint. I signed up for that voice control without question and gave it plenty of space to roam around in my head. It foretold disaster for me from a mile way. The little voice told me time and time again that there was always something to be worried about, especially when it came to my relationships.

Scenario

Let me give you a test drive of exactly how efficient this little voice was for me. Let's say it's Valentine's Day. My husband comes home to greet me with a kiss and a brand-new golden necklace. I should be elated, right? After all, I love jewelry. That little voice inside my head would never allow me to be swayed by such logic or reason. It would sound an alarm at once and trigger a thought flow to go something like this:

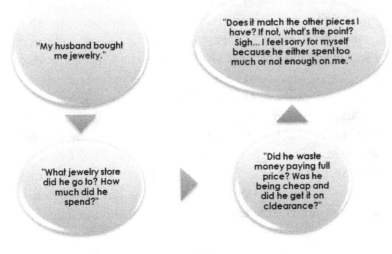

"My husband bought me jewelry."

"Does it match the other pieces I have? If not, what's the point? Sigh... I feel sorry for myself because he either spent too much or not enough on me."

"What jewelry store did he go to? How much did he spend?"

"Did he waste money paying full price? Was he being cheap and did he get it on cldearance?"

Here's what the little voice would say if he did not buy me jewelry for Valentine's Day.

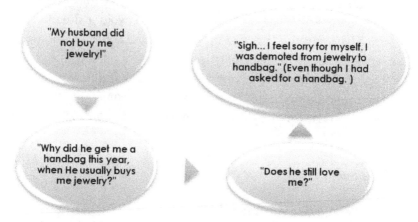

"My husband did not buy me jewelry!"

"Sigh... I feel sorry for myself. I was demoted from jewelry to handbag." (Even though I had asked for a handbag.)

"Why did he get me a handbag this year, when He usually buys me jewelry?"

"Does he still love me?"

When that little voice of negativity and self-pity talks, no matter the scenario, no person can win. If my husband did not buy me jewelry I would wonder, "Well, why didn't he buy me jewelry?" to which the voice would offer many negative responses. When my husband did buy me jewelry I would wonder, "Was it on sale? Is that the only reason he bought it for me? Does he think I'm not worth better jewelry or paying full price?" When I learned that he paid full price I would wonder, "Why did he spend so much money on this one piece of jewelry? If he used coupons or bought the clearance items, he could have bought three pieces of jewelry!" or "Couldn't he find something simpler or on sale? What was he thinking, spending so much on jewelry?" There was no way he could win! There was also no way I was going to win.

Scenarios such as this one are not peculiar to me. They manifest for many people in many ways, but the outcome is always the same: when you heed the subtle voice of Satan your judgement will be clouded with false information, prompting you to carry out actions that are counterproductive to your destiny. That little voice is a demonic one, purposed to get us to a place of isolation. He wants to set you up for a fail by cajoling you to resign to a place of isolation or hopelessness. This leads to stagnancy.

The whole time I thought I had a clever advantage, but in truth, the devil was setting me up! He knew if he could get me to see the worst in people and situations, he could steal my focus and fill my life with fear and sabotage. But how did I ever get to such a place where the devil could so easily deceive me?

HOW TO ESCAPE A SETUP

> *...And that they will come to their senses and escape from the trap of the devil, who has taken them captive to do his will.*
> **2 Timothy 2:26**

The devil set me up for failure the moment I allowed him to answer questions for me. Friends, when you find yourself in a precarious situation—one that forces you or the people who care about you to ask, "Why are you like this?"—get your answer from your manufacturer, not Satan, your accuser! Go to the Word of God and declare His definition of your design over your life. Go to the Lord in prayer and get back to your baseline as a believer!

Identify the things in your life you need to let go of. Such things include ideas and beliefs that are contrary to God's Word. You may need to let go of sin, bad habits, fears, and/or failures—all the things which you know take you to a place of guilt and shame. You need to give them to God and let them go permanently, today. Let the elders of the church pray with you. You don't have to go through it alone. The Lord will deliver you from that maze of confusion, in Jesus' name.

Here are some scriptures you can meditate on, confess, and carry out. These will catapult you out of Satan's setups.

> *They replied, "Believe in the Lord Jesus, and you will be saved—you and your household."*
> **Acts 16:31**

> *He has saved us and called us to a holy life—not because of anything we have done but because of his own purpose and grace. This grace was given us in Christ Jesus before the beginning of time.*
> **2 Timothy 1:9**

> *Truly my soul finds rest in God; my salvation comes from him.*
> **Psalm 62:1**

> *And everyone who calls on the name of the Lord will be saved.*
> **Acts 2:21**

> *For by these He has granted to us His precious and magnificent promises, so that by them you may become partakers of the divine nature, having escaped the corruption that is in the world by lust.*
> **2 Peter 1:4 (NASB)**

No temptation has overtaken you except what is common to mankind. And God is faithful; he will not let you be tempted beyond what you can bear. But when you are tempted, he will also provide a way out so that you can endure it.

1 Corinthians 10:13

Now, those scriptures are a great way to begin climbing out of Satan's snares. How can we recognize the devil's setups ahead of time? In this chapter, we are going to identify the signs and learn to conquer them or avoid them all together.

BAGGAGE

Therefore, since we are surrounded by such a great cloud of witnesses, let us throw off everything that hinders and the sin that so easily entangles. And let us run with perseverance the race marked out for us.

Hebrews 12:1

Imagine being in a crowd of people. Amid the crowd, there is a woman walking towards a bus stop carrying a load so massive, her ability to see is totally impaired. Everyone can see that she is carrying way too much, and it is hindering her ability to navigate forward. Her shoulders, arms, and hands are overwhelmed with a variety of oversized luggage. She is managing several bags of miscellaneous items so heavy that her knees are buckling as she walks! She stops several times, perhaps because her ankles are bogged down by the weight of it all. Imagine this person losing balance and grip, trying to keep everything contained with only her two arms and her strong will. She doesn't take the help of passersby offering to take some of the load off.

A person can have a truckload of negative emotions, invisible to the naked eye, yet quite visible in the realm of the spirit. When you have been carrying the baggage of strongholds, images, and imaginations for so long, you get used to them. You become numb to the burden.

I am a dynamic person who loves the Lord, and I've been like this my whole adult life and for most of my youth. It is possible to love the Lord with all your heart and soul, yet your flesh is still carrying baggage. You would not know it to look at me, but I was once that kind of woman, trying to get somewhere but carrying a load that was impossible for me to bear. For years, I did not know I was tied down by the things I could not let go of. I carried the baggage of offenses, insecurities, fear, and more. People would look at me, thinking I had it all together. But it was only because I had mastered the art of zipping myself up and being cute.

Have you also mastered the art of carrying around zipped, cute luggage? You get the hair done. You shave your beard and put on a well-tailored suit. You get your nails and makeup done flawlessly, and you know the Word of God fluently, but you've not allowed God to get into those innermost places that hurt you. You want to soar like an eagle, but you have weights on you. The only way you can soar is to say, "Lord, yes. It's true. My left wing is strapped down by this five-pound weight, and my right wing is bogged down by ten. My feet are strapped down with chains of fear and regret. Lord, let's break these chains and remove every weight together."

In those days, I could never see hope or glory for the weight of my suitcases full of self-pity, worry, and anxiety. All I perceived were heavy loads of catastrophe and bags of disaster. The weight of those things prevented me from moving forward in faith, in relationships, and even in destiny. What's interesting is—the items in those bags I carried, I never had a true use for them. The things I overwhelmed myself with never came to pass except I triggered them.

Consider this a warning from someone who has been there: When you find yourself feeling overwhelmed, it's time to take stock. What are you carrying that you need to let go of? Let go at once and give it to God! Harboring anything that does not bring you joy or cause you to prosper is a clear sign that the devil is tricking you with overload.

PATTERNS

Yet you say, "Why should the son not bear the punishment for the father's iniquity?" When the son has practiced justice and righteousness and has observed all My statutes and done them, he shall surely live.

Ezekiel 18:19 (NASB)

A variety of imaginations have been passed down from generation to generation and taken from country to country, as migration has occurred. As people have migrated all over the world, negative imaginations have shaped people, nations, and cultures. Unfortunately, these negative images thrive while those affected don't even know.

Check your family history. Check your spouse's history. What is it that has happened before that must not happen to your children? Which parts of your culture or what religious acts have you been taught to exalt above your faith in God? We are going to cast them down in Jesus Christ's name.

Is there a certain time of the year that things always go wrong for you? Is it every time you do intercessory prayer, something bad happens to you? Do you notice that every time you pay your tithes, you get a speeding ticket? These are all traps from Satan to keep you out of covenant with Christ Jesus. Plead the blood of Jesus Christ over such patterns and declare what God has spoken about matters. Change every ungodly behavior or religious act, replacing it with godly character. The devil does not have new tricks, so it should be easy to recognize the snare of generational curses and strange patterns in your life.

HOW TO AVOID A SETUP: LIVE IN THE LIGHT

...For you were formerly darkness, but now you are Light in the Lord; walk as children of Light.
Ephesians 5:8 (NASB)

The most effective way to sidestep the devil's tactics is to live in the light. This occurs when we yield our complete selves to Him. You must yield *all* your thoughts, emotions, desires, and everything else contrary to the life He has granted you. Lay aside everything that gives way to darkness.

The next thing you must do, moment by moment, is renew your mind. This is imperative. Your brain takes in countless images, sounds, and scents on a regular basis. Everything you take in gets processed in your mind. There are images you thought you had dismissed hiding and lurking about in your subconscious. That hidden image will expose itself at the most inopportune time if the devil has his way.

Set your minds on things above, not on earthly things.

Colossians 3:2

If necessary, look in the mirror and declare every good thing recorded in the Holy Scriptures about your life. It does not matter what man has spoken concerning you. I was told, "You're a smart aleck!" I was told, "You won't amount to anything," by people who should have been speaking life to me. God has spoken life into you, just as He did for me. Below are scriptures you must apply to your life routinely before you find yourself entangled in the enemy's snare. The moment you take in something that is not of God, you have a right to reject it.

Imitate God, therefore, in everything you do, because you are his dear children. Live a life filled with love, following the example of Christ.
Ephesians 5:1-2a (NLT)

He answered, "'Love the Lord your God with all your heart and with all your soul and with all your strength and with all your mind' and, 'Love your neighbor as yourself.'"
Luke 10:27

I pray that out of his glorious riches he may strengthen you with power through his Spirit in your inner being, so that Christ may dwell in your hearts through faith. And I pray that you, being rooted and established in love, may have power, together with all the Lord's holy people, to grasp how wide and long and high and deep is the love of Christ, and to know this love that surpasses knowledge—that you may be filled to the measure of all the fullness of God.

Ephesians 3:16-19

You, therefore, will be perfect [growing into spiritual maturity both in mind and character, actively integrating godly values into your daily life], as your heavenly Father is perfect.

Matthew 5:48 (AMP)

CHAPTER EIGHT

HOW TO CAST DOWN IMAGINATIONS

Thy word is a lamp unto my feet, and a light unto my path.

Psalm 119:105 (KJV)

I can't forget the days of looking in the mirror, young, broken, and fearful, wondering, "How does he know I have the eyes of a thief? Can everyone tell that I'm not good and that I should never be trusted?" Even more dreadfully, I wondered, "Am I going to grow up to become a serial killer?" There were times when I thought, just for a moment, that perhaps the world might be a little safer without me. I recall the feeling of my body being overwhelmed with the heavy sensation of gloom.

You may not have had the exact experience that I did, but can you relate? Can you recall, or are you experiencing right now, that stifling weight of both emptiness and heaviness plaguing your mind and soul? I had to cast down every weight of the experiences of my past traumas. If I didn't, only God knows where I would have ended up.

I decree and declare that today is the last day you ever need to feel that way again. For every negative thing that has been spoken into your life that is preventing you from soaring like an eagle, in the name of Jesus Christ, I cast it down and I break it right now!

Now is the time to conquer what's been hindering you. No more waiting. No more excuses. No more entertaining ideas and beliefs that are contrary to victorious living! God has equipped you with everything you need to cast down vain and disruptive imaginations. I am going to give you the three steps necessary to do just that. It is easier than you think, but you must be diligent to carry out all three steps in full sequence. Let's begin.

STEP 1: IDENTIFY NEGATIVE THOUGHT FLOWS

The first step to casting down disruptive imaginations is opening your eyes to see your life as God designed it. How does God see your life? He sees us just as He explained it to Jeremiah, the prophet:

> *For I know the thoughts that I think toward you, says the Lord, thoughts of peace and not of evil, to give you a future and a hope.*
> ### *Jeremiah 29:11 (NKJV)*

If you find thoughts about your past, present, or future projecting anything less than a glorious tomorrow and hope for you, those thoughts and imaginations need to be cast out. Everything God has written in the gospel of your life is good. He knows your beginning from your end, and He planned your end to be glorious. You only need to believe it, decree it, and live it. You are not an accident or a regret in God's eyes. He is an extraordinary strategist! Without infringing upon our free will, He has designed everything to work out for the good of those who love Him—even the bad things![4] God created you because He, as the Great Architect of the universe, decided that without you, the world would be missing something of great value. You matter in the grand scheme of eternity. You cannot allow Satan to manipulate you into believing otherwise.

Thoughts That You Must Cast Down

Here are some examples of the kind of thoughts that must not make your mind their dwelling place:

Proud Thoughts. *Proud thoughts are also called exalted thoughts. Anything you allow your mind to dwell on more than God, or His plans for your life, is an exalted thought. Thoughts of anxiety, depression, and suicide are all examples of the kinds of thoughts that tend to linger in this category. Never think that you know better than the One who created you about your life. Such thoughts must be rebuked immediately.*

Negative Thoughts. *You must cast down every thought and imagination cajoling you to think and act in a manner that is counterproductive to your identity as a child of God. You can recognize a negative thought by the impact it has on*

---

[4] Romans 8:28

your mood and actions. I am going to provide a "Negative Thought Checklist" for you here.

NEGATIVE THOUGHT CHECKLIST

- Do these thoughts cause you to sin?
- Do they cause you to say or do things that go against God's will?
- Do they cause you to experience negative emotions without legitimate cause?
- Do they cause you to feel like all hope is lost?
- Do they cause you to feel like you are alone?

If the answer is yes to any of these questions, the thought must be cast down at once. When such thoughts arise (and they will), you must rebuke them like the lies they are by speaking out the God-given truth, which we will talk more about in Step 2.

Arguments Against the Gospel. If you are a born-again believer in the gospel of Jesus Christ, and you suddenly find yourself questioning God's Word, His promises, and His love for you, know that the devil is at work.

> *We demolish arguments and every pretension that sets itself up against the knowledge of God...*
> ### *2 Corinthians 10:5a*

Every thought disrupting your faith and every thought you have that contradicts the Word of God concerning your life must be cast down.

Hostile Thoughts. In 2003, a study was published in the *Journal of Personality and Social Psychology* detailing the results of psychological tests given to college students after listening to music with violent lyrics.[15] There was a time when people believed that violent music was cathartic, providing an outlet to individuals who needed a safe means to express the hostility of their thoughts. As Christians, we don't need a study to tell us that what we allow to infiltrate our minds and hearts is what will eventually come out.

What are you exposing yourself to? Hostile thoughts are a product of hostile environments. If you are not declaring peace wherever you go, you are invariably accepting and feeding on the hostility of your environment. Hostile thoughts lead to self-destructive, destiny-destroying, and environmentally destructive behavior. Such thoughts will cause you to do or say things that result in harm or violence. When you find yourself faced with such thoughts, do not dwell on them. Conquer them until they never return.

STEP 2: TAKE AUTHORITY | DECLARE THE ANTIDOTE

The tongue has the power of life and death, and those who love it will eat its fruit.
Proverbs 18:21

Did you know that you are a "speaking spirit"? Genesis 1:26 tells us that we are made in God's likeness and image. This is the same God who spoke the world and all its inhabitants into existence. The same tool that God used to set time and space in order is the tool you will use to conquer disruptive imaginations: your tongue. Use the God-given power of your voice to cast disruptions down and to build your spirit up.

Early in this book, I empowered you with the truth: you were born to soar! So, what is weighing you down? It's time to identify it and call it out by name. What has occurred in your past that causes you to feel stifled and unable to open your ears and hearts to receive what the Lord wants to do for you, permanently? Open your mouth and cast it down today, in the mighty name of Jesus Christ!

> "...and we take captive every thought to make it obedient to Christ.
>
> **2 Corinthians 10:5b**

Now, you must take all the thoughts discussed—proud thoughts, negative thoughts, and argumentative thoughts— and say what God has said concerning them. Do not leave any disruptive thought unaddressed. To help you to take action here, I ask that you take a few moments to write those thoughts down right now. I am providing you with a space in this book. I give you full permission, once you have written every negative thought and belief you have about your life and destiny, to tear it out and tear it up, permanently removing it from your life!

List your disruptive thoughts in the column to the right of its respective category. Use the listed scriptures, or add your own and declare it against what the devil has been telling you.

PROUD THOUGHTS	
• Isaiah 29:16 • 1 Corinthians 4:7 • Romans 12:3 • _____ • _____	
NEGATIVE THOUGHTS	
• 2 Corinthians 4:16-18 • Matthew 5:48 • _____ • _____	
HOSTILE THOUGHTS	
• Romans 8:7 • Hebrews 12:3 • 1 Peter 2:21-23 • _____ • _____	
ANTI-GOSPEL ARGUMENTS	
• Ephesians 6:14 • Titus 3:9 • John 14:6 • _____ • _____	

DR. SANDRA OGUNREMI

(Keep adding things here!)

Once you have completed the assignment, the only thing that should be left on the previous page is what God has said concerning your affairs!

STEP 3: PRAISE GOD

> *... Always giving thanks to God the Father for everything, in the name of our Lord Jesus Christ.*
> **Ephesians 5:20**

The final step in eradicating fear and negativity from your life is giving thanks and praise to God. There is power in praise! As you praise God, you are focusing your attention to the only sure, constant source of goodness and mercy that remains forever in existence, and you are partnering with Him. The more you praise God, the more you grant Him permission to work on your behalf.

CHAPTER NINE

HOW TO PULL THE STRONGHOLDS DOWN

For the weapons of our warfare are not carnal,
but mighty through God to the pulling down of
strong holds.

2 Corinthians 10:4 (KJV)

You are five years old when someone tells you that you'll never amount to anything. You remember wondering what that meant and why that would be the case for you, but because you are young and resilient, you move on with your life—that is, until the first time you are reprimanded by someone who says, "What is wrong with you?" The fear of disappointing others sets in. Then you remember, "I was told I would not amount to anything." Learning to tie your shoes becomes a real struggle. The first day of school brings disappointment. You struggle to color within the lines. You get your first assignment back, and it doesn't have the same sticker and smiley face your peers have. Your friends can count much higher than you, and some can even read!

You finally understand what it means not to amount to anything. Now, not only do you understand it, but since no one has exposed you to any other fact concerning the matter, this is what you believe. The day you have your first job interview, you wake up late and everything goes downhill from there for you. A day comes when you have an assignment to complete, and you remind yourself that it was said that you'll never amount to anything. You carry out the task with the mindset of someone who will never amount to anything. This is what it looks like to be under a stronghold. Let's talk more about it.

STRONGHOLD DEFINED

What is a stronghold? Is it the tight grip of sin? Is it a type of demon, perhaps a very stubborn one who just won't leave us alone? No, a stronghold is not a demonic presence. In fact, the Lord establishes Himself as a stronghold for us.[16] How, then, can we describe a stronghold?

A soldier would describe a stronghold as an impenetrable force or fortress the size of an entire city, if not larger. Generally, a stronghold is made effective by both natural and manmade design, making it nearly impossible for the opposition to penetrate while providing refuge for the army to rest, regroup, and execute defensive strategies. A stronghold is more terrible than any form of being, or the degree to which we are bound to something. A stronghold is a fortified atmosphere for fostering a very specific condition that one cannot easily break.

Let's look at some more definitions and characteristics of strongholds. A stronghold is:

A Necessity.

I mentioned earlier that your mind is a battlefield. The devil has made it his highest priority to conquer as much territory in your life and future as you'll allow. If a stronghold is a terrible force, a seemingly impossible-to-conquer fortress, you will need the strongest of them all to defend yourself against Satan's tares. You need the Stronghold, the One who does terrible things in righteousness to protect His children! Let Jesus be your mighty fortress! When the Lord God of heaven's armies is your Stronghold, you can rest assured that you are protected, as He is perfect in all His ways—especially in times of warfare.

An Atmosphere.

A stronghold is an enveloping state that is nearly impossible to break through. When you find yourself in a stronghold, you are not playing on fair grounds. Every experience you have is invariably controlled by the fortified space that you are in. A stronghold differs from other divine artillery in that it consumes every area of an individual's life and fortifies it to withstand any attack.

An Indicator.

Every man is made of three components: a soul (mind, will, and emotions), a body, and a spirit. Your spirit is your eternal essence and it is meant to guide you in life. However, we tend to allow our flesh or body to make our decisions for us. When we do this, it weakens our spirit—or worse, establishes the wrong spirit in us, making our souls ripe for the devil to pick at.

Strongholds are established in your mind, in one way or the other, according to the level of access you have given to a spirit. Understand this: Everything in life is spiritual. What you see and experience now is only because of spiritual activities that have taken place ahead of time. Therefore, your prayer life is so important. We will expound on this shortly.

For now, understand that whatever stronghold is fortifying an area of your life is doing so as a result of the spiritual activities that have taken place in your life. If you are praying in the spirit regularly throughout the day, occupying your time with divinely inspired, God-given assignments, and feeding yourself with the Word of God habitually, you are granting God access to become a fortified city for you. What are you allowing to infiltrate your spirit? This is an indicator of what is fortifying the specific areas of your life.

THE ONSET OF STRONGHOLDS: Trauma

Strongholds are formed at the word of any spirit strong enough and interested enough in protecting its interest. A spirit can only form a stronghold in the areas of your life that are left unprotected, and with your enforcement. If there is an area in your life that you have not guarded with God's Word, you are at risk of a stronghold overtaking that area. Something may have been spoken into your life. Good or bad—if no one has prayed for you in that area or exposed you to God's word concerning that matter, you might take that word of truth into your life, repeating it to yourself over and over, carrying it with you into adulthood. You are reinforcing it. When you agree with that word, a spirit then has license to build a stronghold in you.

Once enforced, strongholds influence your level of expectation, your confession, your habits, and your outcomes in life. Thank God, the "weapons of our warfare are not carnal, but mighty through God to the pulling down of strongholds, casting down imaginations"! (2 Corinthians 10:4-5 KJV). It's the only way to break free from this kind of atmosphere.

Picture This

It is date night. My husband and I are sitting on the couch, relaxed, watching a movie and eating popcorn. Suddenly, I begin to cry. My husband tries to console me, to no avail. He sits there, puzzled and a bit frustrated, as this is not the first time this has happened. "Why?" he asks. "Help me understand." I ask myself the same question, silently, as I suddenly find myself back in my childhood, reliving nightmares of my parents' hostile relationship.

My experience is strange, but not uncommon. In fact, I am sure you can relate. Something is happening, and your body is physically present, but you are completely absent. But this experience I am referring to goes deeper than a wandering mind. The clinical term for it is "trauma induced dissociation." It is a safety response that removes you from situations your physical body cannot handle in the moment. Sometimes your mind takes you to a "safe place," but many times it takes you right back to square one—to the very first time you had such an encounter—because it never really got over it, and it wants you to learn how to respond to it. For many, this experience is devastating. For me, it was destructive.

Let's quickly talk about trauma, as it is a pervasive reality that impacts many if not most people and can lead to self-destructive behaviors if left unaddressed. Trauma refers to one's experience of a disturbing or troubling event that he or she is unprepared for and unequipped for. Trauma has been determined to be imprinted permanently on the brain. It's a scientific fact.

Trauma can be the onset of strongholds. It leaves lasting effects on the brain, specifically the amygdala, hippocampus, and prefrontal cortex. Once trauma penetrates our minds, our emotions are rattled. Our memory can become jarred or distorted. Our ability to take in new information rationally is skewed. You begin to see the world differently, in ways that can trigger the wrong responses to different life experiences.

Naturally speaking, trauma is impairing because when you are overcome with traumatic experiences, that trauma is imprinted throughout your brain. Spiritually speaking, it subjects those areas to what is learned from your imprinter—that is, who or whatever you have allowed your mind and spirit to be exposed to.

Situation	Wrong Response
I have a headache.	What if it's cancer? God, don't let me die! Don't kill me!
Someone who seems more successful than you offers some propaganda contrary to your faith at a time when you feel nothing is working.	Instead of holding fast to your faith, you begin subscribing to false doctrine.
You see your husband talking to a woman.	Lord, please let me live and not die so that my husband won't marry a foolish, evil woman, who will treat my child like Cinderella.

You know you have been exposed to such a situation when, without reasonable, rational cause, you find yourself—a child of God—saying anti-scriptural things.

Believe it or not, I held similar beliefs and prayed ridiculous prayers, all triggered by the trauma of my childhood and how the devil had imprinted in my memory a distorted view of what my life was like. I lived many years afraid that my suffering would be maximized. I married, had my first child, and suddenly I was encumbered with fears for my child and marriage. I believed that things were destined to go wrong. A stronghold and an image can follow you for the rest of your life if you don't pull it down and cast it out!

Perspective | Perception

No matter how glamorously an image is presented to you, your perspective alone determines its value. If an eagle and an ant encounter the image of a sugar cube, the eagle will surely dismiss it, casting it aside, while the ant will put every ounce of energy it can muster into making that image his reality.

Imagine seeing the world and its temptations and trials from the perspective of a small, crawling insect such as the ant. As strong and resourceful as an ant is, everything is still going to feel like an uphill battle for you. There would always be shadows looming over your head. Life would be so laborious, and no matter how much you work and prepare, and no matter how careful you are, there would always be the weight of fear that something could crush you at any moment.

Ants, like all of God's creatures, have purpose and extraordinary abilities, but if I asked you which animal you'd prefer to be, I believe most of us would prefer the majestic vantage point of the eagle.

Before we can cast down these imaginations that have been destroying our lives for so long, we must learn to see them from the right perspective. God has equipped you with a divine position in life, and that position is one of divine advantage. If you are reading this book, I decree and declare that your eyes receive the vantage point of the eyes of an eagle, in the mighty name of Jesus Christ!

THE PULLING DOWN

Like casting down disruptive imaginations, there are steps one must follow to receive total deliverance from ungodly strongholds. Now that we have identified what strongholds are and which ones we need to pull down, let's talk about how to do it.

STEP 1: FORTIFICATION

There is an adage I have heard expressed that has global application and truth. Translated, the proverb counsels, "Prevention is better than cure." In other words, there is always something you can do to prevent encountering situations where such problem solving is needed.

In this case, to avoid exposure to certain strongholds, fortify your life. How? As we learned at the beginning of the chapter, not all strongholds are bad. In fact, Eden, as described in the book of Genesis, was the first earthly stronghold, only broken and dissolved when man chose to step out of it. Otherwise, it protected, preserved, and strengthened man, increasing his power and productivity on the earth.

The LORD is good, a stronghold in the day of trouble, and He knows those who take refuge in Him.
Nahum 1:7 (NASB)

- The Word of God is a stronghold and refuge for you, as it contains God's promises and instructions for your life.

For the word of God is alive and active. Sharper than any double-edged sword, it penetrates even to dividing soul and spirit, joints and marrow; it judges the thoughts and attitudes of the heart.
Hebrews 4:12

- Praise and worship is a stronghold for you. It invites God's presence as an impenetrable force.

Worship the Lord your God, and his blessing will be on your food and water. I will take away sickness from among you.
Exodus 23:25

Sing to God, sing in praise of his name, extol him who rides on the clouds; rejoice before him—his name is the Lord. A father to the fatherless, a defender of widows, is God in his holy dwelling.
Psalm 68:4-5

- The counsel of the godly fortifies you.

  *Listen to advice and accept discipline, and at
  the end you will be counted among the wise.*
  Proverbs 19:20

- Spiritual activity and ministry in the body of Christ
  fortifies you.

  *And let us consider how we may spur one
  another on toward love and good deeds, not giving up meeting together, as some are in the habit
  of doing, but encouraging one another—and all
  the more as you see the Day approaching.*
  Hebrews 10:24-25

  *I will not die but live, and will proclaim what
  the LORD has done.*
  Psalm 118:17

  *So Christ himself gave the apostles, the prophets,
  the evangelists, the pastors and teachers, to equip
  his people for works of service, so that the body
  of Christ may be built up until we all reach
  unity in the faith and in the knowledge of the
  Son of God and become mature, attaining to
  the whole measure of the fullness of Christ. Then
  we will no longer be infants, tossed back and
  forth by the waves, and blown here and there
  by every wind of teaching and by the cunning
  and craftiness of people in their deceitful schem-
  ing. Instead, speaking the truth in love, we will
  grow to become in every respect the mature body*

of him who is the head, that is, Christ. From him the whole body, joined and held together by every supporting ligament, grows and builds itself up in love, as each part does its work.

Ephesians 4:11-16

CALL ELDERS TO PRAY

One of Satan's tactics is to isolate us. He wants us to believe we are alone in our experiences, so that he alone can interpret them for us. If we give him that opportunity, he will translate what could be a blessing into worry, fear, anxiety, or something worse. That's why the Bible gives us this counsel:

Is anyone among you sick? Let them call the elders of the church to pray over them and anoint them with oil in the name of the Lord.

James 5:14

So many people walk alone, carrying their past with them everywhere they go. The Bible says,

Cast your cares on the LORD and he will sustain you; he will never let the righteous be shaken.

Psalm 55:22

You must trust God. Trust that He has gone ahead of you in battle, and trust those He has anointed in the body of Christ to help you in the hard times. Trust His Holy Spirit to lead you to the right man or woman of God who will not only pray with you, but have the authority to lay hands on you and cast down disruptive imaginations and anything else holding you bound, so that you can join the forces of heaven in pulling down those strongholds once and for all.

May the blood of Jesus Christ cleanse your mind of every stronghold and negative influence, in Jesus' name.

CHAPTER TEN

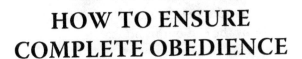

HOW TO ENSURE
COMPLETE OBEDIENCE

We demolish arguments and every pretension that sets itself up against the knowledge of God, and we take captive every thought to make it obedient to Christ. And we will be ready to punish every act of disobedience, once your obedience is complete.

2 Corinthians 10:5-6

Have you "given your life to Christ"? Many of you will answer yes. If you answered yes, yet you find yourself in a perpetual cycle of fear, anxiety, toil, and obscurity, your obedience may be incomplete. You may have made the commitment to surrender your life to God—that is, you agreed to give God your mind, body, and soul. But if you are sincere enough, you may find that you have given Him only one third of your being.

Take a few moments to assess your level of commitment. Do you only obey God to the extent of your convenience? Do you find it difficult to sacrifice anything that feels good to your flesh for the sake of enhancing your relationship with Christ? Is your trust in God limited by your human logic? Do you only trust Him if you feel in control of situations? If your answer is yes to any of these questions, you have not fully surrendered your life to Christ, and as a result, your obedience is incomplete, and the benefits of your Christian life are limited. If this is you, or if you have not given your life to Christ yet, the good news is that you will have an opportunity to make an informed decision about giving your life to Christ by the end of this book.

CHRIST'S OBEDIENCE

Jesus Christ, the Son of God, gave all of Himself for us in obedience to His Heavenly Father.

> *And being found in appearance as a man, he humbled himself by becoming obedient to death—even death on a cross!*
>
> **Philippians 2:8**

It was not only His fleshly body that suffered and died and was buried. His entire being was crucified. His Spirit and Soul descended to the deepest depths of hell to confiscate Satan's authority over death, hell, and the grave by conquering it, and giving us total access to God the Father. The only reason we are eligible for salvation is because of the obedience of Christ. So, to be Christian is to be obedient, fully surrendered to God, our Father, who has called us out of darkness into His marvelous light.

SURRENDER

Now therefore, if you will indeed obey My voice and keep My covenant, then you shall be a special treasure to Me above all people; for all the earth is Mine.

Exodus 19:5 (NKJV)

Surrender is a product of revelation. The moment one realizes that someone stronger and more equipped is destined to win, it is in his or her best interest to surrender gracefully. Failing to do so would be to accept a more violent defeat. As Christ was obedient to the Father, we must yield to Him completely if we want to be Christians, or followers of Christ. We are made in the likeness and image of God, yet we were born into the sinful nature of the world. By default, it is natural for us to want to do things our own way. But consider this: Everything we think, say, or do in appeasement to our flesh is temporal, only sustaining us for a moment in exchange for lasting, negative consequences.

Giving Jesus your heart is not enough. If you don't give Him your mind, your thoughts will eventually guide your flesh to what is counterproductive to the Spirit of God that dwells in you. Hence, a word you must quickly learn to identify with is *surrender*. When you surrender, you commit to give all. You entrust every area of your being to another to manage and handle as desired.

Choosing to surrender your entire life to an invisible God, by way of His Son, Jesus the Christ, is the most important decision you will ever make. If you choose to do so, you are literally exchanging your entire being and agreeing to take His Holy Spirit as your own. Every human is a spirit that lives in a physical body and possesses a soul. If you choose to

141

give Christ your life, you are saying, invariably, that your life is no longer your own. Are you truly willing to give the Holy Spirit complete control of your life? Do you plan to commit to habitual mind renewal, so that the mind of Christ is always in you? If you choose to take on the mind of Christ, you are agreeing to subdue your flesh, bringing it into complete obedience and submission to the Holy Spirit. If you accept the Holy Spirit, but don't take on the mind of Christ or renew your mind daily, you will always be at war with yourself.

You cannot make a decision that will cost you an eternity on a whim or out of due diligence or emotionalism. Now understand this: as a human being, subconsciously or not, you are always operating in obedience to one force or another. As easily as a thirty-second commercial can influence what you choose to have for dinner, everything you allow your five senses to take in touches your spirit, either weakening it or strengthening it. When decision-making times arise, it is the part of you being fed that will be strong enough to influence the decisions you make.

"Why would anyone want to do that?" you may ask. The benefits outweigh the costs. Before you decide who or what you will entrust your life to, you will learn, in this chapter, both the costs and the benefits of putting your life in God's hands by accepting Jesus as your Lord and Savior.

BROKEN JAR

My sacrifice, O God, is a broken spirit; a broken and contrite heart you, God, will not despise.
Psalm 51:17

You ensure your obedience is complete by becoming a vessel with the capacity to carry out God's will. Many of us are broken jars. We are fragile, and our lives are quite fragmented, but we don't want to admit it. We keep everyone at a distance, because from a distance, it looks as if we have it all together. It is only in the hands of God that we can be made whole. It is only in His hands that we can safely remain whole.

So many of us never get to the place where we permit ourselves to be cleansed, repaired, and protected by the Father. Rather than being vulnerable to receive the help we need to be made whole, we invest in our exterior presentation, totally neglecting the inner man which is most important. Jesus pointed this out concerning the Pharisees in the Book of Luke.

> But the Lord said to him, "Now you Pharisees clean the outside of the cup and plate [as required by tradition]; but inside you are full of greed and wickedness. You foolish ones [acting without reflection or intelligence]!
> Did not He who made the outside make the inside also? But give that which is within as charity [that is, acts of mercy and compassion, not as a public display, but as an expression of your faithfulness to God], and then indeed all things are clean for you.
> **Luke 11:39-41 (AMP)**

Man, by nature, is prone to sin, the very substance that gets in the way of our intimacy with God.

These six things the Lord hates; indeed, seven are repulsive to Him: A proud look [the attitude that makes one overestimate oneself and discount others], a lying tongue, and hands that shed innocent blood, a heart that creates wicked plans, feet that run swiftly to evil, a false witness who breathes out lies [even half-truths], and one who spreads discord (rumors) among brothers.

Proverbs 6:16-19 (AMP)

In His mercy, He describes Himself as the Master Potter. He has the authority to mold you into the being He designed you to become. So, we don't need to pretend we are okay. We need to confess our transgressions and our decision to entrust our lives into His hands, so that He can mold us and use us for His glory.

He does not delight in the strength (military power) of the horse, nor does He take pleasure in the legs (strength) of a man. The Lord favors those who fear and worship Him [with awe-inspired reverence and obedience], those who wait for His mercy and lovingkindness.

Psalm 147:10-11 (AMP)

Give Christ your life—broken, fragmented, and all. Admit to Him that you are a mess, but you know He has the power to save, heal, and deliver you. You know that there is healing in Him. Submit to Him so He can mold you back into the divine vessel you are destined to be.

That, regarding your previous way of life, you put off your old self [completely discard your former nature], which is being corrupted through deceitful desires, and be continually renewed in the spirit of your mind [having a fresh, untarnished mental and spiritual attitude], and put on the new self [the regenerated and renewed nature], created in God's image, [godlike] in the righteousness and holiness of the truth [living in a way that expresses to God your gratitude for your salvation].

Ephesians 4:22-24 (AMP)

When our obedience is complete, we are complete. If we follow Christ with our whole heart, He can make us whole and sustain us with the fullness of His grace, mercy, and love.

THE COST OF KINGDOM LIVING

To receive the gift of salvation is free. Jesus Christ paid the price on Calvary. It costs you nothing to receive it. But it will cost you everything to maintain it.

If the endgame of life on earth is obtaining salvation, once we accept Christ, we should just experience a rapture of sorts. This way, we don't risk becoming entangled in the cares of this life or reverting to our sinful nature. If you have given your life to Christ and you are still on earth, you must ask why. There is something on this planet that you are called to do. What is that thing? The only way to know is by asking the One who has predestined your life. Your purpose on earth is to do God's will. You must find out what He requires of you, and follow His instructions for carrying out those assignments.

Yielding

To hear God's instructions and to follow them requires you to yield. You must be willing to stop everything that gives you pleasure, everything that is most comfortable, and everything that has become a habit, so that you can hear God clearly and follow Him. Why would anyone give up total control of his life? The only way it makes sense to do this is when you know the person you are yielding to has your best interests at heart. You must trust God with your life, just as an infant must place his trust in his father or mother to carry and provide for him.

> No one serving as a soldier gets entangled in civilian affairs, but rather tries to please his commanding officer.
>
> **2 Timothy 2:4**

The purpose of your salvation through Christ Jesus is not to make heaven. Heaven is a great benefit, but if it was the only benefit, then once we give our lives to Christ, we should be taken up at once! Instead, we remain here on earth for the sake of carrying out the will of God concerning all the rest of His children, who have yet to come into the knowledge of His everlasting mercy and grace. You literally become a soldier for Jesus, and you must live as such. A soldier never has to worry about what to eat, drink, or wear. They only concern themselves with staying equipped for combat.

BENEFITS OF THE KINGDOM

Before you rethink your salvation, let's look at the benefits of doing something as risky as joining the army of the Lord.

- **Provision:** As I stated earlier, all your needs are met, even before you ask, but your mind must remain on your commander in chief and doing what pleases Him. What are some of the things God supplies to those who enlist?
  - His Presence: You will never be alone or stranded, because He is with you, always.
  - He provides you with revelation.
  - Most importantly, He provides you with the gift of His sweet Holy Spirit. What is so significant about the Holy Spirit in your life? If you yield to the Holy Spirit habitually, it becomes easier to yield and comply, because you learn that He orders your steps and always has your best interests at heart, even when you think you know better. The Holy Spirt is also a Comforter. He gives you peace about situations that under any other circumstances would completely frustrate you. Another benefit of the Holy Spirit is the fruit He allows you to bear the more you listen to Him. You can experience love, joy, peace, and so on, without regard to what is happening around you.
- **Justification:** He justifies you! When you are in Christ, there is no condemnation. You only need to repent, and everything will be all right.

- **New Identity:** The devil may have tricked you into thinking less of yourself. You are made in the image of God! Once you choose to take on your God-given identity, you will be amazed at the seemingly impossible things you can achieve.
- **Renewed Mind | Mind of Christ:** When you think differently, you will feel, behave, and respond differently. As a child of God, you are given the mind of Christ our Savior. That is a mind that sees life in every situation and circumstance, a mind that is focused and purpose driven, a mind that knows the heart of the Father concerning His children, and a mind that knows what to do and when to do it.
- **Authority:** When you join the family of God, you join an unshakeable kingdom. You are joint heirs with Christ, and a royal priest. Jesus said concerning His disciples, "I have given you authority to trample on snakes and scorpions and to overcome all the power of the enemy; nothing will harm you" (Luke 10:19).

WHEN IS YOUR OBEDIENCE COMPLETE?

If you are a Christian, your beliefs, words, and actions should align with the Word of God. Everything you do should be exactly what Jesus would do if He was physically present on the earth and faced with your situation. Your demonstrated integrity is a major indicator that your obedience is complete. How do you know when you are fully surrendered? There are two major indicators. Line your life up with God's instructions. As you pray and receive instructions from the Lord, as you read His word of instruction from the

Holy Scriptures, how exactly do your actions align with His directives?

Integrity: Our Inner Life & Our Outer Life

Our obedience is complete when our inner life matches our outer life. If you invest more time forming the appearance of obedience, you are in danger. When the approval of men matters more to you than obtaining approval from God, you are in danger.

> *I the Lord search the heart and examine the mind, to reward each person according to their conduct, according to what their deeds deserve.*
> **Jeremiah 17:10**

Live with the consciousness that God sees, hears, and knows all. You can deceive people. You can even deceive yourself. But you cannot fool the Maker of all things. God sees your heart, and He understands your intentions. Let your life sustain like a jar. It's okay to be fragile, but like a jar, be clear. Be transparent, and if you're willing to surrender yourself to Him, the Lord will fill you up with content from His heart to yours, so that what is in you will be pleasing to Him as it pours out of you.

> *For the eyes of the Lord range throughout the earth to strengthen those whose hearts are fully committed to him.*
> **2 Chronicles 16:9a**

Love

> *Don't just pretend to love others. Really love them. Hate what is wrong. Hold tightly to what is good.*
>
> **Romans 12:9 (NLT)**

> *By this everyone will know that you are my disciples, if you love one another.*
>
> **John 13:35**

Finally, your obedience is complete when love is your motivator. Religious habit cannot be your motivator, nor can pride, nor can fear. If not going to hell is your only motivation for serving God, your obedience to Him will never be complete.

EPILOGUE

"For God so loved the world that He gave His only begotten Son, that whoever believes in Him should not perish but have everlasting life."
John 3:16 (NKJV)

There is nothing stopping you from soaring higher than you've been able to in times past. Now you know who God has designed you to be, and that He has given you everything you need to overcome. You are fully equipped with everything you need to identify the strongholds in your life and have them broken! For years, the trauma and pain of the negative experiences of the past have weighed you down. But no longer!

YOU ARE NEVER ALONE!

Did you think you were worth less because you were missing a piece of your identity? Do you feel incomplete because you have been told that there is a piece of nurturing, care, or discipline that you were never privy to? Without being fully aware, maybe you have allowed your biological father to define you. Maybe you have been at odds with a mother who breaks your heart repeatedly. If you have been called an orphan or an outcast, now is the time to dismiss every stigma, stereotype, and sentiment of abandonment, and to declare your place as a child loved by the Most High God, who is your Heavenly Father.

The devil wants you to think that you are unlovable and unworthy. He will tell you to settle for whatever kind of affection or human interaction you can get. He will even tell you that you are incapable of expressing your feelings appropriately, or having feelings at all! He has told some people to forget about ever having a family or being a good parent or spouse, because their past has made it impossible for them to care for others. Now is the time to reject and rebuke every stronghold and disruptive imagination attached to such lies! David says in the Book of Psalms,

> *Although my father and mother have abandoned me, yet the Lord will take me up [adopt me as His child].*
>
> **Psalm 27:10 AMP**

Like David, you have the same Heavenly Father, who loves you and who has never left your side!

GIVE IT TO GOD!

If you haven't already, begin to tell the Lord how you feel, and about all the thoughts you have about those situations that have traumatized you over the years, knowing that

He has seen you and He understands, and He has empowered you to overcome! The Bible says,

> *Cast all your anxiety on him because he cares for you.*
>
> **1 Peter 5:7**

The Lord, your God, cares for you, and has preserved you. Whatever has tried to stay in your life as evil, the Lord will turn it around for His glory. Today, I am a different person. I stopped holding on to the things God said we were to give to Him. I stopped fighting the battles God has already sent His Son, Jesus Christ, to win on my behalf, so that I could focus on that which He did call me to accomplish. I should be a woman full of self-pity, unable to be fulfilled, unable to be satisfied, but I am the most joyous human being on the surface of the earth, full of joy, full of gratitude, full of thanksgiving for what God has done for me.

YOU ARE THE AUTHORITY!

I should have been a downcast, self-pitying, relationship-sabotaging wreck the remainder of my days here on earth. But I found out that I was not limited to the boundaries of my circumstances. I am the authority. God gave me dominion, and everything I need, to live life the way He created me to live. So, I took all that Satan meant for my evil, and I turned it around by the power of the Holy Spirit. God is using my past to help others with their present and future state. Your hands have also been anointed to war![5] All the things you've never being able to get rid of—today, it's

---

5   Psalm 144:1

time to say, "No more! I pull down the stronghold of low self-esteem! Stronghold of addiction, I pull you down! Be cast out, in the mighty name of Jesus!" Take authority over every demonic imagination! The strongholds of darkness that have been looming over your life are pulled down now, in Jesus' name!

ALTAR CALL

It is my prayer that you are moved to enhance your relationship with your Maker. It is why you were created. In fact, if you are reading this book right now and you are not in a covenant relationship with God the Father, through Christ Jesus, His Son, and with the gift of His Holy Spirit, I must extend the opportunity to you right now to do so. The rest of the information in this book is useless to you if you don't know Jesus Christ as Lord and Savior, because casting down imaginations requires you to know God. As I mentioned earlier in this book, you were created to soar. Today, in the name of Jesus Christ, those weights will be permanently broken. If you are ready to make this commitment, or you know in your heart that you must rededicate your life to Christ, say and believe the following:

> *Father, in the mighty name of Jesus, I accept You as Lord and Savior of my life. You have the power to save, heal, and deliver, and I am a sinner in need of salvation that only comes from You. Lord Jesus, I believe that You were born, You lived, and You died on the cross and rose again to deliver us from the bondage of sin.*

If you confessed this prayer, congratulations! Welcome to the family of God. You now have access to all the promises of God, and you are in prime position to know Him better and better.

Defend Your Victory

Satan has already lost the battle. Jesus has already won the victory for you. All you must do is defend it! This is the major work of casting down disruptive imaginations and the pulling down of strongholds. There's no physical fight, especially if you understand that the end is already established. All you need to do is walk in your victory.

Psalm 23 describes this best. You may need to "walk through the valley of the *shadow of death*." But the key word is *shadow*. You don't need to give death any attention. Satan uses such shadows to distract and discourage you.

Jesus has already won the battle over death, hell, and the grave. You only need to walk through it with confidence that God is with you and that He has already won. That feeling of defeat we feel sometimes is an instance of Satan trying his best to drown us in disruptive imaginations, so we can't see that it is over, that it's the dawn of a new day—a day when you will fly on eagle's wings.

The Lord has set a table for you in the presence of your enemies. He has even made them your footstools. In other words, every challenge you face can only work in your favor. May the Lord open your eyes to see His greatness, His grace, His love, and His protection over your life and destiny, more clearly than you see any shadow of darkness today, in the name of Jesus Christ. Remember, you have the power to cast down every disruptive imagination!

ENDNOTES

1 © 2019 Merriam-Webster, Incorporated
2 www.zooborns.com
3 Genesis 2:7
4 Genesis 2:8
5 Genesis 2:22
6 Psalm 38:4
7 Genesis 2
8 PTSDUnited.org
9 John 8:44
10 Genesis 1:3
11 Proverbs 4:7
12 Acts 1:8
13 Through Ishmael, the faith of Islam was birthed.
14 Genesis 17 promise given to Abraham | Genesis 21 Promise materialized when Sarah conceives Isaac| Genesis 35 promise fulfilled through Jacob
15 *Journal of Personality and Social Psychology*, May 2003. News release, American Psychological Association © 2003 WebMD, Inc. All rights reserved.
16 Nahum 1:7, ESV

ABOUT THE AUTHOR

Dr. Sandra Ogunremi is an ordained minister with the Assemblies of God churches. She has served as the Black Hills Sectional Representative for the Women's Department in South Dakota since 2008. She teaches on the importance of love, laughter, and life. She has taught throughout the United States, Canada, Africa, and England. She derives great joy and fulfillment when motivating, inspiring, and coaching others. She coaches people on alleviating hurt, pain, and the anguish that can sometimes leave people emotionally crippled. She speaks on living a meaningful life while being physically and spiritually healthy. She is happiest when she is being used as a conduit to bless others.

She has been married to Dr. Ayodele Ogunremi, a board-certified nephrologist, since 1993, and they have three adult children.